Handy Learning

Activities
for
Hand Development
and Curriculum Enhancement

Published by:
Handy Learning Seminars, Inc.
P.O. Box 270688
Flower Mound, TX 75027

Copyright and Reproducing

Photographs have been used with permission.

Notice:

Neither the publisher nor author assume any responsibility for any loss or injury and/or damage to persons or property arising out of or related to any use of the material contained in this book. It is the responsibility of the treating practitioner, teacher, or parent to rely on independent expertise, knowledge, and judgment to determine the best treatment, appropriateness of activities, intervention, and method of application for the patient, student, or child.

Author's Note

It is hard to believe my first edition of this book was written over fifteen years ago. Yet, the content remains relevant today, despite the dramatic technological changes that have occurred.

Some may believe that handwriting will become a lost art and fine motor skills are no longer important as we move more and more toward keyboarding and voice recognition technology. But handwriting is deeply rooted in our human development. Handwriting is integral to our need to communicate. It is through handwriting that we learn and remember. Even if handwriting plays a secondary role in the future, we will continue to require fine motor skills for our daily lives and self expression.

The use of our hands will never be outdated. We use our hands to engage upon the world in a three-dimensional way. We are humans, and those appendages at the end of arms; our hands, are still very much needed in our daily lives. We use our hands to eat, to create, to communicate through gestures, to organize our environment, to dress and complete our self-care.

In many ways, it is through the very use of our hands that we express our humanity. No other mammal on this earth uses a body part to create and engage in the world as we do with our hands.

Susan offers on-site training and workshops on hand development and implementation of the Handy Learning program. To find out about upcoming workshops, please email handylearninginc@gmail.com. For course outlines and offerings please visit Handylearning.com.

Our hands put us in touch with the world.

Susan Thomopson, OTR

Handy Learning

TABLE OF CONTENTS

Introduction

Most children are starting school with underdeveloped hands yet are pushed to higher curriculum expectation levels each year. The result is poor habits due to weak hand muscles that later become habituated and unchangeable. By second or third grade, these children are holding their pencil with a maladapted grip and producing illegible, nonfunctional handwriting.

Handy Learning addresses this problem by bridging this gap. *Handy Learning* is a proactive program that provides children with activities that strengthen and prepare their hands for the tasks demanded of them at school.

Handy Learning promotes fine motor development while supporting academic goals through activity-based learning. The children benefit by learning key educational concepts while simultaneously developing hand skills. The coupling of fine motor tasks with academic goals, makes *Handy Learning* unique, fun, and successful.

Handy Learning educates parents and teachers about hand development and provides accessible activities that can be easily set up at home and in the classroom. All of the activities have been piloted for years and are child driven. The activities are fun to the child. He will engage in the activity readily with attentiveness and motivation.

Through *Handy Learning* your child or student will develop foundational hand skills so that he will be ready for the fine motor demands of school. Some of these school skills include holding a pencil, writing, drawing, pasting, coloring, and cutting with scissors. Good habits will be formed from the onset because his little hands will be properly prepared!

> In a pilot case study, after daily exposure to the ***Handy Learning*** program, 95% of students with disabilities were able to naturally (without instruction) hold their pencil with a tripod grasp and were able to draw developmental strokes by age five.

ATTENTION: Some of these fine motor activities include small parts. Young children should be supervised during these fine motor activities.

Academic Goals

Handy Learning activities were designed to correlate with curriculum guidelines. Teachers will find *Handy Learning* easily integrated and supportive of curriculum standards, goals, and objectives for a wide range of students.

Curriculum topics include:
- Language and Early Literacy (including prewriting)
- Mathematics
- Science
- Social Studies
- Fine Arts
- Personal & Social Development
- Physical Development
- Technology Applications

Handy Learning activities provide the classroom teacher with a means to provide daily fine motor activities yet integrate these activities to support a variety of the above listed curriculum content areas.

A Child's Occupation

Just as adults have "occupations," children do, too. Occupations are how we fill our time and include all activities that give us meaning and purpose in life. Adult occupations include work, leisure, and maintenance activities. An adult may engage in a myriad of occupations throughout their day including going to work, taking care of a child, and expressing oneself through a craft or hobby. Occupations serve to define who we are and what is important to us. Occupations develop us as humans.

Children have two primary occupations: play and student. Both occupations are integral and essential to development. As a child plays, he is developing and learning through the three-dimensional exploration of the world.

Take for example a child that is playing in a sandbox. Through this one activity he is developing physical, sensory, and cognitive understanding. Let's take a look at this seemingly simple activity:

Sandbox Sam:
As Sam runs his hands through the sand he is activating his sensory system and stimulating his touch receptors. He is discovering sensory sensations such as the feel of the grainy sand in his palms, the coolness of the sand against his legs, and the weight of it in his hands.

As he digs and cups the sand with his hands, Sam develops and strengthens the arches and small muscles of his hands; all prerequisites to holding a pencil correctly. When he pours the sand from containers he learns about quantity, weight, and volume on an experiential level that he understands. Another child may be with him and he engages in creative and dramatic imagination as Sam makes up games with his friend, burying dinosaurs and excavating "bones."

Sam is fully engaged in an activity of play that teaches him about the world and stimulates his brain systems on many levels. The occupation of play is his teacher.

As a child attends school he develops his mind and body through the challenges and demands of the occupation of being a student. He begins to move from concrete, three-dimensional learning to the more abstract, cognitive process of learning. He continues to develop throughout his academic career.

The Environment of Today

Our environment can either serve to facilitate or hinder our occupations and development. Small environmental changes can either promote success or in some cases, impede success. For example, one would not attempt the refined fine motor task of embroidery while using knitting needles (incorrect tools) under poor light (hindering environmental influence). This would clearly be a frustrating and unsuccessful venture. There are usually specific tools best suited for specific tasks.

Today's environment has changed the way people and children engage in occupations. Despite the advantages of some environmental changes, there are some drawbacks. Being aware of how the environment impacts child development is an important knowledge base that a parent or teacher can use to influence child success.

In following pages, four examples of how environmental changes in our society have affected child development will be covered. While they are not the sum total of environmental influences on development, they each carry a significant role in the decline of hand development in children.

They are:

1. Sudden Infant Death Syndrome (SIDS)
2. Baby carriers
3. Passive entertainment
4. Increased expectations

www.handylearning.com

1. SIDS

Another environmental influence on child development has been the reaction to Sudden Infant Death Syndrome. Because of SIDS, babies are positioned on their back when they sleep—"back to sleep." However, as a result, many babies spend an inordinate amount of time on their backs and never have the opportunity to be prone on their tummies.

The prone position is integrally important in the development of children in many ways. Because developing children are not having the opportunity to be on their tummies, delays are becoming more apparent when they enter school.

When a baby is prone, he learns to prop, first on his elbows and then on his hands. This serves to promote development including visual development, body awareness, upper body strength, and hand development.

Within the hands are many tiny receptors. These receptors become activated during propping or bearing weight through the arms and hands. Some receptors of the hands receive information about touch and some about joint-sense.

The joint-sense receptors are called *proprioceptors*. Proprioceptors are activated through weight bearing and are important in the development of the small muscles of the hands called *Intrinsics*.

Intrinsic muscles allow for refined, precise movements of the fingers. They also are responsible for building the overall structure of the hands. In fact, intrinsic muscle development is so important, that the intrinsic muscles are loaded with more proprioceptive receptors than our trunk and limbs combined. This is because intrinsics are essential to the development of fine motor skills.

With prone positioning and weight bearing through the hands, proprioceptors are stimulated. As the proprioceptors are stimulated they send messages to our hands and brain that result in strengthening of the hands, development of hand arches and balancing of muscles in the hands. These components set the stage for future development of refined fine motor skills.

Proximal means toward the center of the body. Another important benefit to propping is it develops *proximal stability*. Most proximal muscles and joints serve to provide a stable foundation for fine motor skills. Propping strengthens these proximal muscles including the arms and shoulder muscles.

When a baby pushes up on his arms while prone, he is working against gravity and sustaining contraction of postural muscles in his arms and shoulders. By propping, these muscles develop strength. They eventually develop to provide a stable base for the hands to work freely and precisely without the need for external support. All fine motor movements must occur with a good stable base, or good proximal stability.

Finally, when a baby props up on his arms while prone, he increases his visual field and creates coordination between his neck muscles (that are working against gravity) and his eye muscles (ocularmotor). This muscle and neurological combination is working to develop future skills of visual motor tasks such as reading, drawing, and eye-hand coordination activities.

www.handylearning.com

What you can do

It is developmentally important for babies to spend time on their tummies. Tummy time will help to develop the hands through weight bearing. It will also help to develop visual motor skills through neck extension and will develop proximal stability through upper trunk extension and weight bearing through the arms.

You can facilitate all of this by simply positioning your baby on his tummy during playtime. Keep this adage in mind:

"Back to Sleep; Tummy to Play."

2. Baby carriers

Another way our environment is changing the way our children develop is through the use of baby carriers. Baby carriers have been designed for safety, comfort and convenience. In the past twenty years, there has been an increase in a variety of containers in which to place, carry and hold babies. In fact now days, a baby can be transported throughout the day in a carrier across several environments. He can be transitioned from the car to the grocery store and to a restaurant without ever disturbing his position.

As wonderful as this is for the parents, too much use of a baby carrier is not a good thing. The baby carrier removes several developmental opportunities including the development of the *vestibular* system, body awareness in space, visual field and tracking, and postural stability through the development of the trunk and neck muscles.

Let's compare a baby who is carried on the mother's hip (Baby Anna) versus the one transported in the carrier (Baby Beth).

<u>Baby Anna</u>

Baby Anna is picked up from the car seat and taken into her mother's arms. During this transition, Baby Anna's middle ear is sensing the movement and sending messages to her brain about where her body is in space. Her trunk muscles respond by flexing and extending according to where her head is during the transition. Baby Anna looks for her mother and locks her eyes onto her mother's face, exercising visual tracking.

Baby Anna is rested on the hip of her mother. She smells the closeness of her mother and feels the warmth of her mother's body against her own skin. She feels her mother's cotton blouse brushing against her legs. Her mother's long hair wisps against Baby Anna's cheek, making her giggle.

Now upright, Baby Anna looks around with wide eyes as her mother walks across the parking lot. As she turns and looks different directions, she rotates around the center of her body, the midline. She learns where her midline is by moving and turning to see the world.

Baby Anna feels the rhythm of her mother's steps through her body. Her proprioceptors are stimulated by this input. The forward movement stimulates her middle ear and visual system offering information of where she is in space. With her mother's stride, Baby Anna is constantly making small postural adjustments to stay upright.

As her mother waits to be seated at the restaurant, Baby Anna sees something and reaches out, extending her arm against gravity. She is motivated to explore her environment. She opens and closes her little fingers in anticipation. Her curiosity is peaked. Someone standing next to Baby Anna smiles and coos at her, making her smile in a social response.

Baby Beth

Baby Beth lounges restfully in her carrier. She is on her back (supine) and so does not have to work her trunk muscles at all. She receives limited sensory information because most of the input is to her back, which has few receptors.

Because she is down deep in the carrier, her visual field is limited. It is as though she has side blinders on. When she looks up, she sees mostly the ceiling of buildings. There is little to occupy this active, seeking mind. Occasionally, Baby Beth reaches out toward an interesting item. However, her reach is limited by her position, and she is unable to make contact with her hands. She closes her hands and curls them close to her body.

Baby Beth's middle ear is being stimulated as the baby carrier gently sways during the stroll across the parking lot. However, because her body muscles are not engaged, she is not able to interpret the middle ear input for body awareness in space. Once at the restaurant, Baby Beth falls asleep. Her curiosity and social responses are limited.

What you can do

Be aware of the amount of time your child spends in a carrier. Build some time in for carrying your baby. Facilitate curiosity and engagement with other people and your baby's environment while carrying your baby in your arms.

3. Passive Entertainment

Today, technological advances provide heightened entertainment and ease of lifestyle. These inventions have changed our environment, our expectations, our performance, and ultimately our occupations.

Children's toys have dramatically changed in the last ten to twenty years, therefore changing the way children play. The bulk of what is available today is push-button electronically driven toys. These toys require few hand skills and decrease active engagement with the environment. Unfortunately, children are readily drawn to the trance of this "passive" entertainment.

How does this impact the occupation of play and a child's development? Compare what Vincent gains through playing a video game versus that of Sam in the sandbox:

Video Vincent

While playing a video game, Vincent receives no sensory information other than visual and auditory feedback. None of his foundational sensory systems are being stimulated. As he plays, he is sedentary and still, requiring few responses to challenge his somatosensory brain development. He receives no feedback for body awareness in space or developing the muscles of his body.

The video game offers no dimensionality, or tangible experience in terms of weight, volume, and position in true-life space. Vincent's hands are not receiving any type of tactile feedback nor are they challenged in terms of muscle development.

Vincent is so focused on the game and in his own world that his sister nearby goes unnoticed. He is unaware of social opportunities occurring around him.

Because the game is creating a scenario for him, Vincent's creativity is staunched. No imagination is necessary. It is as though he is performing the all-important, developmental occupation of play in a vacuum.

Unfortunately, this analysis is true of computers and TVs as well. While children may learn cognitive skills such as math and reading from computers, the real world three-dimensionality function of play is lost.

What you can do

As a parent you have the ability to choose and set up the environment in which your child grows and develops. By designing the environment to facilitate appropriate engagement in the occupation of play, you are promoting readiness skills including mental, physical, and sensory development in your child. You are being a powerful instrument in the successful development of your child.

Work to create an environment full of opportunities for three-dimensional play. Limit the amount of passive entertainment available to your child. Replace passive entertainment with active entertainment.

Your knowledge of the environmental influences and the occupation of play will serve to properly prepare your child for his next occupation—that of student.

4. Increased expectations (Too much, too soon)

In today's society the mindset seems to be about getting ahead. Often parents interpret this mindset by exposing their child to a variety of different opportunities and activities at a young age. Exposure is important in promoting talents and skills in your child. However, it is just as important to balance the exposure and expectations of a child with what is developmentally appropriate.

In child development, there are optimal windows for growth. Exposing the child to an experience he is not developmentally ready for is forcing an issue before the window is open. It only causes frustration and in some cases, the formation of bad habits. Bad habits are formed because the child wants to succeed and so attempts the activity by compensating for what is not yet developed.

A prime example of this is encouraging the child to write letters and draw shapes before he is developmentally ready. Young children are being pushed to write their names even at the age of three years old! This is simply not appropriate. The typically developing child does not have the hand musculature or visual-motor skills to produce written letters. This scenario is not unlike asking a child to run before he can walk.

If the child does happen to learn writing his name at an early age, the skill is acquired from rote teaching and not from true learning. A skill attained through rote teaching is called a *splinter skill*. A splinter skill is not transferred to other skills and does not facilitate further learning. A splinter skill is not a true form of learning. Rather it is only a result of focused training. In addition, because the child is compensating for building blocks that are not yet in place, he can form bad habits such as holding the pencil incorrectly and forming letters incorrectly. The result is a trained habit that he will most likely carry with him to and throughout school.

Instead, it is much better to focus on the developmental building blocks of hand development and fine motor skills before requiring the complex task of writing and drawing. Then when it is developmentally appropriate to learn to write (around age five or six) he will learn the skill quicker and with greater success. In addition, he will be able to transfer his skill to writing other words and letters. He will efficiently learn to write without a struggle.

The primary window for hand skill development is ages three to five years old. It is during this time that the child is developing dexterity of the fingers and the use of the hands for fine motor manipulation. The small muscles of the hands are acquiring all of the actions that will later be essential to holding a pencil and making the small, precise movements necessary to form letters. These muscles are developed and trained by engaging in a variety of daily fine motor activities. It is through these activities that the child will be prepared and ready for picking up a pencil, holding it correctly, and forming letters with fluid movement and precision.

What you can do

Allow your child to explore coloring, drawing, and writing as he is developmentally ready and not before. Educate your private schools and other parents to the importance of teaching writing only when the child's hands are fully developed and when it is developmentally appropriate.

The Write Stuff
A recipe for success!

The Write Stuff

Rome was not built in a day. Neither are hands!

There are many elements of foundational hand development required before placing a pencil in children's hands and expecting them to write effectively. All too often, however, children are pushed to skip these foundational skills and jump directly to writing before the child's hands are ready.

Without the Write Stuff (foundational hand development) the following often results:

- **The "Funky" Grip**—the child's hands are not developed or strong enough to hold a pencil correctly and produce the precise movements required for writing. Therefore, the child grabs the pencil in any way possible, desperately seeking control and stability. The result is a Funky Grip (which is *not* functional) that becomes habituated. By the time the child has developed hand musculature and structure for holding a pencil correctly, he has practiced the Funky Grip to the point of an unbreakable habit. Once in third or fourth grade, the student begins to struggle with the increased writing demands and their writing becomes sloppy or illegible.

- **Manipulation**—If a child's hands are not ready for writing, he will avoid writing. Often what we interpret as negative behavior is really fear, frustration, and avoidance. If you aren't a good

runner, you won't like to run and will avoid it whenever possible. And so it is with a child who has underdeveloped hands—he will not like to write or draw. Acting up in class is a better alternative to failure or humiliation.

- **Drawing Letters**—Developmentally, the child lacks the ability to produce the refined pencil movements required to write the letter strokes and doesn't have the visual-motor understanding of developmental strokes. So the child, desperate for success, draws the letters in a piecemeal, nonflowing manner instead of writing the letters with proper letter formation and strokes. For example, she begins all of her letters from the bottom up. Her circles are clockwise instead of counterclockwise. Her lowercase "d" might look like an odd curlicue formed from the bottom up, her lowercase "a" is a poorly shaped basketball with a vertical stick somewhere loosely in the vicinity of the ball. By first grade, these letter formations are habit. By third grade they are not just a nuisance, but result in overall illegible handwriting and frustration.

"a"

"d"

"b"

"+" not
crossing
midline

The Write Stuff Ingredients

The following pages will cover all of the key foundational hand skills required to be able to hold a pencil and manipulate it with skilled precision for the task of handwriting. These ingredients are also necessary for successfully engaging in all fine motor tasks in life. Daily fine motor tasks include dressing, eating with utensils, cutting with scissors, performing self care tasks such as brushing teeth, opening bottles, milk cartons and food bags, zipping, buttoning and snapping, and many more that we tend to take for granted throughout the day.

Building a foundation
- Proximal Stability
- Distal Mobility

Hand Function and Structure
- Hand Arches
- Intrinsic Hand Muscles
- Extrinsic Hand Muscles
- Hand Separation
- Pronation/Supination
- Wrist Extension
- In-Hand Manipulation Skills
- Tripod Grasp

Other Ingredients
- Sensory Processing
- Visual Processing

Instructions:

Take the following ingredients, mix well with daily activities, and baste with positive reinforcement!

Building a Foundation

Proximal stability and distal mobility are foundational ingredients on which all the other fine motor skills are built.

Proximal Stability

Proximal is a term that means "toward the center" or the midline of the body. A stable base is provided through stability of the trunk and shoulder muscles, or the proximal parts of the body. The trunk, neck, and shoulder muscles work together to create an upright and stable posture. This stable posture is needed so that the fingers have a solid platform to perform precision movements.

Proximal stability is the foundation to developing good fine motor skills. Imagine yourself attempting to thread a needle while sitting on a large ball with your feet off of the ground. You have no solid base of support, no proximal stability. Can you see how difficult it would be to thread that needle?

Now imagine yourself threading the needle seated in a chair with your feet on the floor and your back up against the back of the chair. You might even prop your elbows on the table in front of you. You thread the needle in half the time and with half the effort. This is because you created a stable base, or proximal stability, from which to perform the fine motor task of threading the needle.

Shoulder stability; Arms are away from her trunk.

This child has good **proximal stability**. She is able to maintain an upright, stable posture while sitting without external support.

For some children who have underdeveloped proximal stability, performing fine motor skills feels like threading a needle while sitting on that ball. It is important to develop proximal stability in the child.

What you can do

As mentioned before, proximal stability is developed through positioning so that the baby or child bears weight through his arms and hands. Allow your child to play on the floor. Set up Handy Learning activities on the floor. Your child will naturally prop on one or both arms while on the floor and will be building proximal stability.

Another option is to place activities on a vertical plane. For example, pin up butcher paper on the walls for tracing stencils, or place a pegboard on an easel. Placing fine motor tasks on a vertical plane forces the child to lift his arm against gravity and stabilize the shoulder muscles. Placing the item on a vertical plane at or above eye level increases the demands on the shoulder muscles.

A great example of a fine motor toy designed on a vertical plane is the Lite Brite.

Distal Mobility

Distal means toward the extremities or ends of our body, like the fingers. When a child writes letters by moving the pencil with the fingers, he is demonstrating "distal mobility." Distal mobility cannot be achieved without proximal stability as a platform. We build precision at the fingertips by having a good solid base of support through proximal stability. Thus the saying: "Mobility on Stability."

Distal mobility is facilitated primarily through in-hand manipulation tasks. These tasks require intrinsic muscle involvement and small motor movements of the fingers.

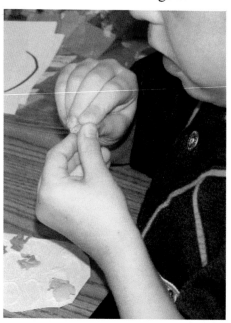

Distal mobility

The Size of Toys and Pencils

It is important to realize that in-hand manipulation skills cannot be acquired by using the large objects that are most readily available to children. The items or manipulatives must be scaled to the hand size and thus, smaller for the child.

Imagine yourself attempting to turn over an item in one hand in order to inspect it. Which would be easier for you to turn in one hand, a quarter, or a large jar lid? The quarter would be easier. While turning the quarter over, you are using the small, intrinsic muscles of your hand which are designed for creating the precise movements required in handwriting. However, in turning over the jar lid, you are most likely using the larger muscles of the hand called *extrinsics*. These muscles are *power* muscles and are not precise in function.

In order to develop the precision muscles of the child's hand, the object must be scaled down to the size of the child's hand, thus relatively small. Only then will the intrinsics be targeted for development.

Small toys for small hands!

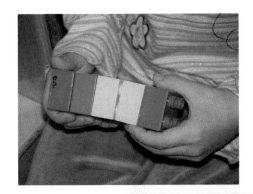

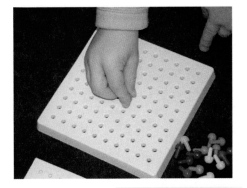

Too big!

Compare how the small pegs above facilitate the small muscles as opposed to these large pegs on the left.

Unfortunately due to litigation and liability, small items for children are not readily found. Please note that because of the need for intrinsic, distal involvement, many of the Handy Learning activities include small parts and as a result, children do need supervision.

What you can do

Set up the environment of play to include small manipulatives. Expose your child to small pegs, Lite Brite, broken pieces of chalk and crayons. Broken pieces of chalk and crayons facilitate a tripod grasp because the child does not have enough material space to hold the implement incorrectly. Do not use large diameter pencils, crayons, or chalk.

Practice buttoning and unbuttoning, snapping and unsnapping during dressing times. Use lacing cards for lacing and stringing beads no larger than ¼ in. Most importantly, supervise your children during these small manipulative activities! See the Activities section of Handy Learning at Home for more ideas.

Hand Function & Structure

The following are various hand structures and their respective functions. These structures are later referred to in the Activities section. Understanding these functions will allow you to choose a specific activity to support the development of specific hand structures in your child.

Hand Arches

Like the foot, the hand has arches. These arches provide stability within the hand so that refined movement at the fingertips can be accomplished. Without this internal hand stability, the hand is "floppy" or "soft." The hand arches provide a stable platform to perform controlled movement at the fingers.

What you can do

Hand arches are best developed through weight bearing and fine motor manipulation activities. Hand arches can also be developed by scooping and pouring with the hands, sand, rice, or beans. Other techniques for developing hand arches are described in the Tactile section under Activities.

Intrinsic Hand Muscles

Intrinsics are the muscles are primarily responsible for producing legible handwriting. These muscles are located inside the hand and do not cross the wrist. They are the fine, small muscles of the hand which allow for refined precision and control. They can move in intricately and they gain feedback for providing just the right amount of force and speed to accomplish a required fine motor movement.

The intrinsic muscles of the hand include the Interossei, Lumbricals, and the muscles of the Thenar and Hypothenar eminences. Each of these muscle groups are discussed in more detail in the following section.

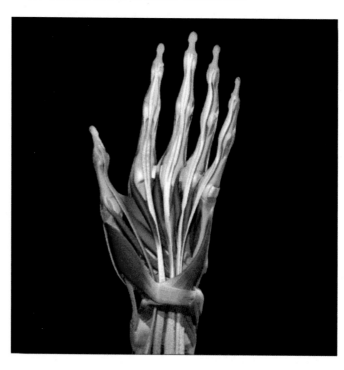

Photo used with permission from Primal Pictures

The intrinsic hand muscles include the following muscles and functions:

Interossei and Lumbricals

These are small muscles positioned between the long bones in the palm of our hand. Their primary function is to provide small, refined movements of the fingers required for dexterous tasks. These muscles give us precision and the right amount of force to complete fine motor tasks.

Thenar Eminence

The thenar eminence is the main muscle belly of the thumb. It includes three intrinsic muscles and allows for thumb opposition. It is considered a "skilled" muscle rather than a "power" muscle. It is the main muscle set for holding and moving a pencil in a tripod grasp.

Thumb opposition

Thumb opposition is the ability to oppose or touch the thumb to all of the fingers. Thumb opposition is essential to being able to hold and manipulate a variety of objects and school tools.

Hypothenar Eminence

The hypothenar eminence is the muscle belly of the little finger. It allows for opposition with the pinky and includes two intrinsic muscles.

What you can do

Most of the activities in Handy Learning are geared toward intrinsic muscle development. Engage your child in these and other similar activities. Also provide plenty of weight bearing opportunities to activate the receptors of the intrinsic muscles.

Extrinsic Muscles

Extrinsic muscles are the muscles located outside the hand. These muscles are in the forearm but have tendons that cross the wrist, and go to the fingers.

Extrinsic muscles tend to be "power" muscles and are most often used for gripping large or heavy items. When you carry a piece of luggage, you are using some of your extrinsic muscles to maintain the grasp around the handle. Extrinsic muscles tend not to be precision muscles and function more for power and stability.

Extrinsic muscle development is important in maintaining wrist extension during fine motor tasks. See Wrist Extension below for more details.

What you can do

Children most often develop the extrinsic muscles through their gross motor play such as climbing, crawling, pulling, and swinging. Any form of sustained, strong gross grasp is exercising the extrinsic muscles. Most important for fine motor skills is the extrinsic positioning and stabilizing of the wrist. More details on the importance of wrist extension will be covered in the Wrist Extension section.

Hand Separation

The hand can be separated into two sides with two different functions. One side, the pinky and ring finger, offers stability. These fingers are often tucked or curled into the palm when performing fine motor tasks to provide stability. The other side, the thumb, index, and middle finger, perform manipulation skills such as writing with a pencil or buttoning a button. The development of hand separation is crucial for fine motor control.

This boy's right hand is demonstrating good hand separation as he crinkles small pieces of tissue paper.

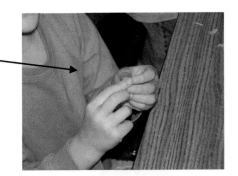

This child doing the same activity but has no hand separation.

What you can do

You can facilitate hand separation by teaching your child about the different functions of the hand. Make up a name for the stabilizing side of the hand, such as the "Secret Side" and explain that those fingers hide inside the palm of the hand; that is the Secret Side's job.

To further aid in the development of hand separation, have your child hold a makeup wedge or other small item in the Secret Side of the hand during fine motor activities. This will force the hand into its two separate functions of stability and mobility.

An activity that inherently promotes hand separation is cutting with scissors. However, the scissors must equal sized and small loops for the fingers. Unfortunately the scissors commonly found in classrooms has one loop larger for the fingers. These are counterproductive to developing hand separation.

Have your child hold the make up wedge with the Secret Side of the hand and manipulate the scissors with the thumb and middle finger. The index finger should be positioned outside of the scissors for stabilization of the scissors. The child will now be cutting while using and developing hand separation.

See Teaching Cutting Skills for the sequence in teaching your child how to cut successfully.

This child has finger flaring while cutting; a common symptom of poor hand separation.

This child is demonstrating good hand separation during cutting. Do you see his "Secret Side" tucked into his palm?

Benbow scissors are designed to promote hand separation; there are two small loops for the fingers.

These scissors do not promote hand separation because all of the fingers fit in the bottom large loop.

One solution is to turn these type scissors upside down to promote hand separation.

Pronation/Supination

The ability to turn the palm upwards toward the ceiling is called supination. Turning the palm down toward the floor is pronation. Positioning the hands in partial supination during fine motor tasks is considered a mature motor pattern, while a pronated hand position during fine motor tasks is considered more primitive.

Palm down ☹

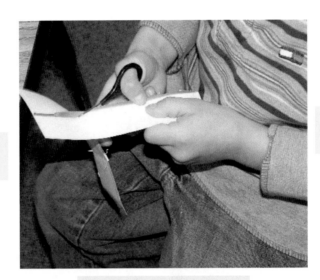

Palms up ☺

Pronated cutting

Supinated cutting

What you can do

Look at your child as he laces a lacing board or cuts with scissors. Does he hold the lacing card with his palms primarily facing up (supinated), or with them facing down (pronated)? If your child is using a pronated approach to cutting or holding the lacing card, simply sit behind him and reposition one or both of his forearms. Gently rotate them so that his palms are facing more toward the ceiling instead of down toward the floor. You may have to reposition the lacing card or paper in his hands so that his palms are facing up while holding the paper.

Wrist Extension

Wrist extension is the best position for hand function. Wrist extension is when the hand is slightly bent upward (the back of the hand toward the forearm). Stable wrist extension facilitates refined movements and control at the fingertips. A wrist that is floppy or flexed downward (wrist flexion) does not provide the stability needed to perform fine motor tasks. Wrist extension is achieved primarily through the extrinsic muscles which have tendons crossing the wrist. Because these tendons cross the wrist, wrist extrinsics help to stabilize the wrist.

Wrist extension is brought about by placing the manipulative on the floor—this is the same as a vertical surface.

Wrist extension on a vertical surface.

What you can do

Have your child draw, color, or paint on a vertical surface. This promotes wrist extension. It is difficult to paint or draw on a vertical surface without the wrist in the proper position of extension. Another alternative is to place fine motor activities on an easel. Working on the floor also promotes wrist extension as well as proximal stability. Try to limit working, drawing, writing at a desk and choose the floor or easel instead.

In-Hand Manipulation Skills

There are different types of in-hand manipulation skills. One is the ability to move a small item from the palm of the hand to the fingertips without assistance from the other hand. Another is the ability to rotate or move items (like a quarter) around the fingers from index to pinky without the assistance from the other hand. These movements are performed with the intrinsic muscles of the hand and are key to being able to make the different strokes needed for writing letters and numbers.

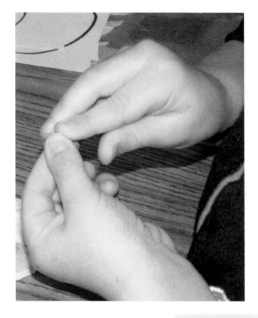

In-Hand Manipulation skills are being used to form this small ball out of tightly rolled tissue paper (on left) and Play-Doh (on right).

What you can do

Engage your child in Handy Learning activities.

Observe how your child performs a fine motor task and watch for compensating or "cheating" such as stabilizing the bead on the table when stringing beads instead of holding it in his hand, or holding the fine motor item up against his body to stabilize the item instead of moving it with his fingers.

Tripod Grasp

The tripod grasp is the preferred functional grasp for holding a writing implement. It is formed by placing the index, thumb, and middle finger in a triangle-type grasp to hold the pencil (see photo above). To adequately form a tripod grasp, all of the foundational components must be well developed.

What you can do

Use small broken pieces of chalk or crayons to facilitate the development of a tripod grasp in young children.

Develop the proper musculature and foundational skills for holding the writing implement by adequately exposing the child to fine motor activities that develop the hands. Do not push the child to write before his hands are ready!

Other Ingredients: Sensory and Visual

Sensory Processing

The sensory system is a complex neurological response to stimuli in the environment. Sensory processing occurs when external stimuli is taken in and organized for functional outcomes.

For example, in order for Johnny to write down his assignment, he must see the paper, feel the pencil in his hand, hear the teacher's instructions, sense his body in space and stay upright in his chair, filter out irrelevant noises and sights, and motor-plan through the letter formations. A seemingly simple task is complex in sensory processing demands.

Appropriate sensory processing must be in place in order for the child to learn and glean information from his environment. Sensory processing typically develops along with other systems in the child through the occupation of play.

The following offers brief descriptions of sensory skills that are required for the skill of writing. This description is merely an introduction to sensory function. For more detailed information concerning sensory processing, refer to the Resources section of this book for references on this topic.

Proprioception

Proprioception is the ability to feel one's own body position in space. There are a multitude of nerve endings in our joints and muscles called proprioceptors. These receive input when the joints are compressed from gravity, deep pressure or heavy work activities like jumping. They in turn, offer feedback to sense where our body is in space.

Vestibular

The vestibular sense is activated through our inner ear and eyes. It helps us with balance, our sense of movement, and knowing where our body is in space. It is stimulated by swinging, riding a bike, jumping on a trampoline, or any other movement that activates the inner ear. Our vestibular center helps us to organize and interpret sensory information.

Tactile Discrimination

Tactile discrimination is the ability to feel and discriminate tactile qualities. The hands have many touch sensors. This sense of touch and the ability to interpret it accurately is integral to performing fine motor tasks.

Kinesthesia

Kinesthesia is the ability to feel and sense one's own body as it moves through space. Body awareness in space is integral to developing concepts such as boundaries and visual perceptual skills.

Kinesthesia can be used for teaching a new skill. Kinesthetic learning tends to "stick" with a person better than other forms of learning. For example, you have heard that once you learn to ride a bike, you never forget. This is because learning to ride a bike is done primarily through kinesthetic feedback. Because it is learned kinesthetically, it is well ingrained.

One method of teaching handwriting is through kinesthetic methods of learning letter formations. Children learn to form letters with their eyes closed. They learn how the letter feels instead of relying only on how it looks. In this way, the child learns the letter formation quicker and more permanently. This technique is used in the *Loops and Groups* cursive writing program by Mary Benbow, OTR. See Resources for more details.

Crossing Midline

This is the ability to cross over an imaginary line running through the center of our body. A child with midline problems will often switch hands depending on which side the marker or crayon is placed. He will not reach across the imaginary line through the center of his body.

The ability to cross midline is important in developing efficient motor patterns and establishing hand dominance as well as the ability to draw letters. A child with midline difficulties may draw a cross by drawing the horizontal line as two separate lines, one on each side of the vertical line.

Not crossing midline while drawing a cross. Three different strokes instead of a horizontal line crossing over the vertical one.

Bimanual Hand Use

The use of both hands in a lead-assist relationship. Usually one hand stabilizes the task (holds the paper) while the other manipulates the task (cuts the paper).

Bilateral Integration

Bilateral integration is a sophisticated combination of sensory processing. If the child's sensory processing is developed properly, the child will be able to coordinate the two sides of the body to accomplish functional tasks in a sequential manner.

Motor Planning

Motor planning is the ability to perform a novel motor task without difficulties and transfer the learned movement patterns to a new task. Motor planning is required to learn and remember any motor task.

Graded Movement

Graded movement is the ability to predict and control the force and rate of movement necessary for a task. A child with poor graded movement may appear clumsy, uncoordinated, and "hyper." They might write letters impulsively and quickly and with poor legibility.

Visual Processing

Visual Acuity

Visual acuity is the ability to see things clearly. It includes distance and close vision as well as depth perception.

Visual Perception

Visual perception is the ability to see, discern, and recognize shapes visually. If a child does not accurately perceive a square, then he cannot draw a square. The child uses visual perception to recognize subtle differences between letters such as an "f" versus a "t" or a "t" and an "x."

Visual Motor

Visual motor skills are the ability to draw or reproduce what one sees. Visual motor skills are also involved in activities such as copying block configurations, tracing along a maze, and cutting along a line. Without visual-motor-skill development, the child will struggle to write letters.

Developmental Strokes

Developmental strokes are basic drawings that a child should be able to perform before expecting them to write letters. They include, in order of development: a vertical line, a horizontal line, a circle, a cross, a square, two diagonals, an "x," and a triangle. **These are prerequisites to developing good handwriting!**

Diagonal strokes are the most difficult, therefore the "x" and the triangle are the last to develop.

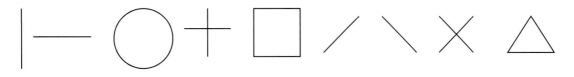

These are all the ingredients to developing the Write Stuff. With these foundational components in place the child will have the ability to write legibly and automatically. He will learn with ease.

Attempting to skip over these building blocks will be counterproductive. Your child might have some immediate success but the long range success will be hindered without the appropriate foundational skills in place first.

Implementing Handy Learning

Handy Learning can be implemented to fit any style of teaching and can be set up in a variety of settings. It can be used in the classroom, at home or in a therapy clinic. The following section offers examples on how to set up the Handy Learning activities in different ways and in different settings.

Avoid changing center activities too frequently as repetition is key to success and development. In addition, selecting a balanced variety of centers is most important. In other words, selecting three activities which all target the same muscles would not be beneficial. Whereas, selecting a tactile activity, an intrinsic muscle activity, and a writing activity would provide a balanced approach.

Handy Learning in The Classroom

If you are a STRUCTURED TEACHER, you might try it this way:

- *Set up a maximum of three centers around the room*
- *Set a timer for 7 minutes*
- *Have two to three students per center with one adult at each center when possible*
- *Have the students rotate at the timer*
- *You can do this on a daily basis or alternate with Gross Motor Lab – i.e. Gross Motor Lab on Monday, Fine Motor Lab on Tuesday, etc.*
- *Repetition is important so try not to change out centers too frequently. For example, introduce one new center with two old ones*

Sample Plan:

WEEK 1 –
1. Tongs- Sorting fuzz balls with picklers, strawberry hullers, tweezers, etc.
2. Stereognosis Box – matching items, naming items.
3. Play-Doh Fun – snipping and cutting Play-Doh and rolling into small balls.

WEEK 2 –
1. Continue with tongs
2. Continue with Play-Doh
3. Water Play

WEEK 3 –
1. Continue with Water Play
2. Toothpicks and Styrofoam
3. Continue with tongs

If you are a LESS STRUCTURED TEACHER, you might try it this way:

♦ *Have centers out as a permanent and integral part of the room setup. Allow students to play with center items on free will and through self-exploration. Rotate items throughout the year.*
♦ *Have centers as part of "free-play".*
♦ *Have a center time and allow students to self-select and rotate at own pace.*
♦ *Place items/bins on a student accessible shelf, such as tong box, tactile bin, etc. Use picture symbols on the bins so that students are familiar with contents.*
♦ *Use spontaneous, activity-based intervention to teach and target goals by referencing this book for Developmental Goals for each activity.*
♦ *Go with the flow!*

OTHER IDEAS:

Have a "Magic Suitcase"—Rotate different fine motor lab centers/items in the suitcase. Allow students to open and discover what "toys" are in the suitcase for the week. Kids love the suspense! Get a suitcase with lots of zippers and they will be working zipping/unzipping as well. Have a daily Magic Suitcase time.

Gross Motor Lab/Fine Motor Lab—Rather than have students sit idle waiting their turn during Gross Motor Lab, have the students work on a Fine Motor Lab activity. They can rotate between Gross Motor Lab activity and Fine Motor Lab activity and never be sitting without something to do!

Include the Parents—Make copies of the activities for the week and send them home so that the parents can see what you are doing and possibly do some of the activities at home.

Handy Learning in Your Home

Children with fine motor delays may exhibit avoidance behaviors toward fine motor activities. It is therefore important that the Handy Learning activities be set up so they are integrated into your child's daily occupation of play. Handy Learning will work best if the toys and manipulatives are imbedded into the child's play environment.

Try not to make the Handy Learning activities structured assignments, homework, or exercises. Rather make it so that the child engages in the activities in a natural, unforced manner.

Handy Learning activities have been piloted and proven to be child driven. There will be something that your child likes and will engage in willingly. Even if your child plays with just a few of the Handy Learning activities, he will still be strengthening his foundational hand skills.

Environmental Designer

As the designer of your child's environment, you may want to introduce only a few of the Handy Learning activities at a time, controlling which activities your child engages in. The following are suggestions on how to introduce Handy Learning activities into your child's environment. Be as creative as you like or as nonstructured as you like. The importance is the exposure and play that your child is being afforded, not necessarily the format.

Avoid changing activities too frequently as repetition is the key to success and development. In addition, select a balanced variety of activities. In other words, selecting three activities which all target the same muscles would not be beneficial. Selecting a tactile activity, an intrinsic muscle activity, and drawing activity provides a more balanced approach. Use the list under "Targeted Fine Motor Development" to determine the best combination of activities for a balanced approach.

Engage your child in all aspects of play, not just the fine motor component. Encourage your child as he uses his imagination, curiosity, and language skills to discover and learn while playing with the Handy Learning manipulatives. Most importantly, have fun while your child participates in the important occupation of play!

Now let's read how Hanna has discovered Handy Learning:

Hanna Discovers Handy Learning

Hanna is a quiet four-year-old girl who has spent the bulk of her life inside the house. She doesn't like outdoor activities and prefers to watch cartoons on the television. Hanna does have a few dolls that she likes to play with. One doll cries when you squeeze its hand and the other doll moves its arms and legs when a button is pushed. Because Hanna's toys are designed for safety, all of Hanna's toys are larger than three inches, requiring a gross grasp on most everything.

Hanna has "soft" hands with poor arch development and "mushy" muscle structure. She does attempt to color with a crayon but bores of it quickly and complains that her hand hurts when she colors. She holds the crayon with a fisted grasp because it is easier that way for her. She shows no interest in attempting to draw lines or shapes.

Hanna's mother decides to change Hanna's environment to facilitate hand development. Hanna's mother realizes that play is an important developmental occupation for her child and that what is in Hanna's environment has an impact on how Hanna develops. She remodels Hanna's play environment to better bring about developmental play.

Hanna's mother first looks for a vertical surface in Hanna's room. She decides that the side of the play refrigerator will work well. She paints the side of the refrigerator with chalkboard paint and transforms it into a black chalkboard. She places broken pieces of chalk in a plastic mug next to the chalkboard. She says nothing to Hanna, wanting the process to be one of discovery, novelty, and excitement for Hanna.

Next, Hanna's mother buys Play-Doh and a plastic bin. She puts rolling pins, old child scissors, a plastic knife, a Play-Doh extruder, dough stampers (available through Lakeshore—see Resources), and a broken pencil, in the plastic bin. She puts an old vinyl shower curtain on the floor in Hanna's room to protect the carpet from dropped Play-Doh. She places the Play-Doh Fun bin on the floor for Hanna to discover.

In another corner, Hanna's mother sets up a Lite Brite on a high surface so that Hanna has to stand while playing with the Lite Brite. This will work her shoulder and trunk muscles more for developing proximal stability.

Finally, she makes another bin full of kitchen tongs and tweezers with a variety of small to medium items to pick up. She puts a few plastic cups in the bin so that Hanna can sort items or place them in different cups while using the tongs to pick them up. She places this bin on the floor so that Hanna will play on the floor while using the tongs.

 www.handylearning.com

Hanna's mother places smaller Handy Learning items in a "Magic Suitcase," an old suitcase that she never uses. She puts various Handy Learning activities in the suitcase for Hanna to discover as a treasure in her room. Hanna will have to unzip and zip the suitcase in order to get to the items, thus working on the self-care task of managing zippers. The suitcase will be "Magic" because the items in the Magic suitcase will change as her mother swaps things out when Hanna is not around.

Hanna's mother has effectively set up the environment for discovery, fun, and developmental play. Hanna is excited to find new toys in her room and now spends more time playing than watching her cartoons. She often takes her mother by the hand and shows her what she is doing, asking her mother, siblings, and friends to play along with her. She is immersed in a three-dimensional play situation that excites her, engages her and provides growth and development in a natural way—through her occupation of play.

Getting Organized

The following materials are needed for Handy Learning activities. Most are available at general stores such as Walmart*. In fact, you may find that you have many of these items in your household already. A shopping list is provided in the next section to make it easier for you to obtain the materials needed for Handy Learning.

If it is an item that can be obtained through a catalog, the company is listed after the item. Company names and ordering information are located in the Appendix and on the shopping list. However, vendors change often so please rely on a Google search of the keyword as you look for items.

After you purchase the items, organize them in the suggested plastic bins. You will need four sweater bins and six shoe-box bins. I recommend the Sterilite sweater bin and the Rubbermaid shoe-box bin, both available at Walmart. In the section, Handy Learning Materials, there is a list of what each bin should contain.

Items are constantly changing, discontinued or carried by different vendors. **Please rely on a Google search using the keywords provided.** If you still can't find an item, feel free to email me (email address is in front of this book).

Also please remember NO SUBSTITUTIONS OR ADDITIONS!! All of these activities have been researched for their effectiveness. Substituting or adding only dilutes the effectiveness of the Handy Learning Kit!

Important note:
Finally, the materials list and activities are the "meat and potatoes" of my hard work over the last fifteen years. Please do not make copies and distribute. If you like the contents and the program, then I ask you to support me and the program by recommending the book to others. Copying or reproducing any portion of this book is agains copyright law.

* I do not have an association or benefit from any of these suppliers. These materials and suggestions are made out of years of investigation, trial, and error. I have found that these items are durable, reasonably priced, and that children are motivated to play with them.

Handy Learning Materials

Four Large Plastic Containers:

PLAY-DOH BIN:
- Scissors
- Lakeshore alphabet dough stampers
- pattern rolling pins
- Dough extruder (spaghetti maker)
- plastic knife
- pencil without lead

BIRDSEED TACTILE BIN
- This is regular wild birdseed available at Walmart
- Letters from alphabet beads

WATER PLAY BIN
- Small squirt bottles—Walmart pharmacy
- Squeeze toys—Oriental Trading or U.S. Toy
- Small baster—Walmart
- Sponges torn into 2-3" squares
- Plastic Baby syringe— Walmart pharmacy
- Plastic eye droppers— Walmart or Therapro

Fine Motor BIN I
- Lacing cards
- Brilliant Builders (connector straws)
- Get a Grip On Patterns Pegboard
- Rubbing plates

Handy Learning Materials

Six Shoe-box Plastic Containers:

Tong Box
- Pom-poms
- Small erasers for sorting
- Koosh balls
- A variety of tongs – medium to small size
- Pickle grabbers
- Strawberry huller

Nuts 'n Bolts
- Real nuts and bolts ¾" or larger
- Threaded PVC piping for screwing and unscrewing

Penne Pasta
- Yogurt containers with holes poked into the tops

Fine Motor BIN II
- Squiggle pen
- Alphabet stringing beads
- Child's first stencils
- Pegboard set

Fine Motor BIN III
- Stamps and stamp pad – tall narrow stamps
- Wikki Stix
- Wooden clothespins and index cards with numbers or letters on them for matching clothespins to cards

Handy Learning Materials

<u>Other Handy Learning Items:</u>

- Lite Brite
- Magna Doodle
- 3-way tabletop easel
- Cutting Kit - See Cutting Kit section of this book for items
- Toothpicks and Styrofoam with basic homemade pattern cards
- String-Along or Filo set
- Lumi Board

Handy Learning Shopping List

WALMART
Wild birdseed *(10-pound bag)* *(Pet supply)* for <u>TACTILE BIN</u>

In Grocery:
Rice or beans for <u>TACTILE BIN</u>
Penne Pasta – <u>paired with yogurt cups with holes on top</u>
Straws for <u>CUTTING KIT</u>
Colored toothpicks to go in Styrofoam

In Toys:
Play-Doh Fun extruder *(makes spaghetti out of Play-Doh)* for <u>PLAY-DOH BIN</u>
Lite Brite
Magna Doodle and/or Aquadoodle

In Pharmacy Department:
Small squirt bottles with trigger pull *(travel section)* for <u>WATER PLAY BIN</u>
Tweezers—squeeze and scissor type *(cosmetics)* for <u>TONG BIN</u>

In Housewares:
6 Rubbermaid shoe-box plastic containers
4 Sterilite sweater-box plastic containers
Small baster for <u>WATER PLAY BIN</u>
Nonslip drawer liner (for putting under Lite Brite)
Wooden clothespins
Small and large index cards for <u>CUTTING KIT</u>
Sponges—½ in. thick *(household cleaners)* for <u>WATER PLAY BIN</u>

HARDWARE STORE
Nuts and Bolts (no smaller than ½ in.)
PVC pipe and threaded receivers

Handy Learning Shopping List
Catalog or Internet:

Discount School Supply
http://www.discountschoolsupply.com
Stamp pad
Brilliant Builders (connector straws)
Pattern rolling pins for Play-Doh Bin
Dustless chalk
2-sided mini-chalkboard
Rubbing plates
Economy tabletop easel
Animal-shape stencils

Lakeshore Learning
http://www.Lakeshorelearning.com
Alphabet Dough Stampers
Stamps for Play-Doh Bin
Lakeshore Pipe Builders
Lace-A-Word beads
Indestructible Lacing Cards Set

Fun and Function
http://www.funandfunction.com
Feel and Find
Squiggle Wiggle Writer pen
Wikki Stix

Amazon
http://www.amazon.com
Appetizer tongs
Pickle grabbers
Metal strawberry huller
Ice tongs
Bamboo tongs 6-1/2"
Amco Stainless Steel Mini Serve Tongs

Other Sources for Tongs
http://www.pocketfulloftherapy.com
Alternate source for pickle grabber

U.S. Toy
http://www.ustoy.com
Mini Erasers (*optional*)
Squirting water toys

Oriental Trading
http://www.orientaltrading.com
Porcupine toys (balls) for Tong Bin

Therapro
http://www.therapro.com
Plastic Eye Droppers for Water Play Bin
Get a Grip On Patterns Pegboard
Peg-It Therapy Tool
String-Along Lacing kit or Filo (*must have for tripod grasp!*)
Wind-up toys

47

Handy Learning Activities

Each Handy Learning activity has a general description and two lists. The lists assist in choosing what activities are best for the child to support the child's development. The "Learning Goals" list relates directly to Kindergarten curriculum goals. The other list, "Targeted Fine Motor Development" relates how that activity targets specific hand skill development.

Targeted Fine Motor Development:

Targeted Fine Motor Development identifies what specific hand structures and skill is developed by the activity. Use this list to help to determine a good balance of activities. Allow the child to self-direct and engage on free will. If the child prefers certain activities over others, this will still be beneficial as all of the activities are designed for fine motor development.

Learning Goals:

If the child is above Kindergarten age, you can take the general concept and make it more challenging. For example, promoting developmental strokes is one Learning Goal for the chalkboard activity. If the child is in first grade, you would want to increase the Learning Goal to write letters of the alphabet or write short words and sentences instead of simple developmental strokes. Most of the Learning Goals can be upgraded to more difficult levels.

Handy Learning Activities

The *Handy Learning*© activities are arranged in the book in alphabetical order:

Chalkboard
Clothespins
Cutting Kit
Feel 'N Find
Hole Punch
Lite Brite
Macaroni Bin
Magna Doodle
Nuts n' Bolts
Pegboard
Picture Lacing Cards
Play-Doh Fun
Squiggle Pen
Stamps
Stencils
Stereognosis Box
Straw Connectors
Stringing Beads
Tabletop Easel
Tactile Bins
Tongs
Toothpicks and Styrofoam
Water Play
Wikki Stix

CHALKBOARD

Description of Activity: Chalkboards offer more kinesthetic feedback than paper or dry-erase boards. In addition, they do not have the odor that dry-erase-board markers carry. For children with breathing sensitivities or allergies, there is Dustless Chalk. Because of the feedback, **children learn drawing and handwriting at a faster rate when using chalkboards**.

Allow the child to explore on his own, copy, imitate, draw dot-to-dot, or trace through mazes. **Use small broken pieces of chalk to facilitate a tripod grasp.**

Targeted Fine Motor Development:
- Tripod grasp
- Visual-motor coordination
- Visual perception
- Wrist extension
- Proximal stability
- Crossing midline
-

Learning Goals:
- Developmental strokes (vertical line, horizontal line, cross, X, circle)
- Shapes, letters, and numbers
- Holding writing tools
- Left to right progression

Suggested Positioning: Children should work on a vertical surface. Either place the chalkboard on the floor or on an easel. Another option is to find a wall or other vertical surface to make a chalkboard. Lowe's or Home Depot carries chalkboard paint that transforms any flat surface into a chalkboard. Also available is chalkboard contact paper. This contact paper can be affixed to any smooth surface and can be easily moved and used again. See Shopping List or Resources.

CLOTHESPINS

Description of Activity: Clothespins **must be held correctly** to strengthen the skilled muscles. If the clothespins are held in the typical, incorrect way, the power muscles are strengthened instead of the skilled muscles. Please refer to photographs for the correct clothespin grip. In addition, please refer to the "Positioning" below so that this activity will be best set up for reinforcing mature motor patterns.

Clothespins offer a myriad of activities and are readily available. Wooden ones are best because they can be marked with letters, colors, shapes, or numbers for matching, spelling, or doing math.

Here are a few clothespin activity suggestions:

- Use clothespins to attach matching playing cards together
- Write letters on ends of clothespins and have your child spell words by clothes pinning on the edge of an upright umbrella
- Create a cardboard dinosaur and have your child place clothespins on the dinosaur back to create the dinosaur "spines and horns"
- Sort shapes by clothes-pinning like shapes together
- Clothespin items from smallest to largest
- Hang up play clothes with clothespins and sort according to color or attire (pants, shirts, jacket, etc.)
- Sort and clothespin pieces of cloth by texture
- Pick up items with clothespins as you would tongs
- Use number flashcards and have your child place the correct amount of clothespins around the lip of a can
- Write numbers or letters on the clothespin
    - Your child places the clothespins on a sheet of cardboard in sequential order
    - Match lowercase letters on clothespins to uppercase letters on cardboard
    - Complete simple math equations with numbered clothespins
- Create a color pattern for the child to repeat

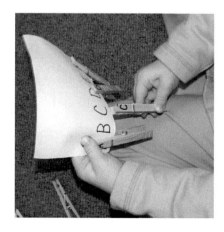

Photo 1

CLOTHESPINS, continued

Targeted Fine Motor Development:

- Hand separation/arches
- Tripod grasp
- Intrinsic muscle development
- Thumb opposition
- Motor sequencing
- Visual perception (matching shapes, etc.)
- Forearm supination/pronation

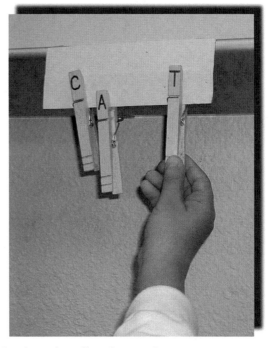

Photo 2

Learning Goals:

- Colors
- Shapes
- Matching
- Sorting and grouping
- Numbers and letters
- One-to-one correspondence/counting
- Sequencing and patterning
- Seriation (small to large, etc.)
- Descriptive Qualities (with fabrics—soft, fuzzy, checkered, polka-dot, etc.)

Positioning: Have your child grasp the clothespin with his first three fingers and his thumb on top (see photo 1 & 2). Facilitate hand separation by having him hold onto a makeup wedge or other small item with the Secret Side of his hand. Do not allow for positioning as in photos 3 & 4.

Place the target where the clothespins will be placed, at or above eye level, to facilitate supination (palm up) rather than pronation (palm down).

Incorrect grasp is pictured in photos 2 and 3.

Correct grasp is pictured in photos 1 (prior page) and 4.

Photo 3

Photo 4

www.handylearning.com

CUTTING
(refer to Teaching Cutting Skills for more information)

Description of Activity: The child cuts various media according to skill level to develop cutting skills. Media is roughly graded from easiest to most difficult as follows. Lines can be added to any of the media to increase visual-motor skills.

- Cutting straws
- Snipping Play-Doh
- Snipping index cards
- Cutting card stock strips 1 in. width
- Cutting index cards
- Cutting half page of card stock
- Cutting full page of card stock
- Snipping regular paper
- Cutting half page of regular paper
- Cutting regular paper

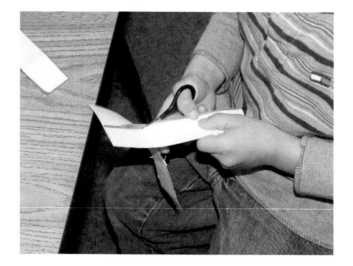

Generally, the thicker and the smaller the media, the easier it is for the child to cut. Benbow scissors are highly recommended to encourage proper hand placement during cutting. See your campus OT to acquire these scissors.

Targeted Fine Motor Development:
- Eye-hand coordination
- Bilateral integration/sequencing
- Hand separation

Learning Goals:
- Manipulate school tools
- Sequencing (motor)
- Visual-motor skill development

Suggested Positioning: Do not allow the child to stabilize their trunk against the table or to prop their arms on the table during cutting. Elbows should rest at their side and not be stabilized against their trunk. The dominant hand should be in wrist extension NOT flexion. The assist hand should hold the paper with the palm side up.

FEEL 'N FIND

Description of Activity: These are simple wooden one-piece puzzles. They can be used in a variety of ways and are extremely versatile. Here are some sample uses:

- Use in Stereognosis Box—place puzzle on top of box and have student find corresponding puzzle piece by feel alone
- Have students trace or draw the selected puzzle pieces
- Place only basic puzzle pieces (circle, square, etc.) in Stereognosis Box or Tactile Bin. Have students find a puzzle piece and then draw on the chalkboard what they found
- Use puzzle pieces to teach shapes (find the circle, square, etc.)
- The more puzzle pieces out at once, the more the student must visually scan and discriminate between objects
- Sort by color
- Group by color, animals, shapes, etc.
- Hide puzzle pieces in Rice or Birdseed Bin

Targeted Fine Motor Development:
- Tactile discrimination (imperative for learning)
- Hand translation skills

Learning Goals:
- Understanding qualities of size, shape and texture
- Learning shapes (circle, square, triangle, etc.)
- Describing attributes/similarities and differences
- Sequencing (find the duck THEN the square)
- One to one correspondence/Counting
- Grouping/Sorting
- Matching
- Orientation (place the duck BEHIND the square)
- Part to whole

HOLE PUNCH

Description of Activity: The student uses a hole punch to punch out shapes from a piece of paper. The hole is punched by squeezing a lever down once the paper is in place. Have the students alternate squeezing the lever with their thumb and first finger, then thumb and middle finger, and so on. This helps to develop the small muscles of their hands as well as thumb opposition.

After the shapes are punched, more advanced students can pick the shapes up with tweezers and glue them onto paper.

Targeted Fine Motor Development:
- Intrinsic muscle development
- Thumb opposition
- Hand arches/separation
- Visual-motor skill (gluing the shapes in a maze, or on a line)

Learning Goals:
- One-to-one correlation
- Counting
- Sequencing
- Orientation (place the shape ON the line, UNDER the line, etc.)
- Left to right progression

LITE BRITE

Description of Activity: The child places small bulbs in holes with patterned paper to form shapes. Thinner paper can be used to make it easier. You can draw basic designs or shapes for the child to follow on black construction paper or regular white paper.

Targeted Fine Motor Development:
- Hand separation (little finger and ring finger tucked under);
- Hand arch development
- Tripod grasp
- Wrist extension
- Shoulder girdle and proximal stability
- Eye-hand coordination and visual perception

Learning Goals:
- Shapes and colors
- Horizontal, vertical, diagonal lines, cross, and X
- Left to right progression
- Sequencing and patterning (red, yellow, blue, red, yellow, blue)
- Orientation (top, bottom,
- middle, above, below)
- Size—small circle/large circle
- Counting; one-to-one correlation
- First and last; more/less
- Numbers and letters

Suggested Positioning: The child can be seated, kneeling at a child-sized table, or standing for this activity. Do not let the child lean against the table! Place nonslip material under the Lite Brite. Place bulbs in a small bowl or plastic butter dish.

Supervision recommended due to small parts and electric plug.

MACARONI BIN

Description of Activity: The child takes small elbow macaroni and inserts them, one at a time, through a resistive hole in the top of a plastic container such as a yogurt dish. Make the hole in the top of the plastic lid by punching it with a pencil. The hole should provide just enough resistance to make it challenging.

Draw different shapes/numbers/letters on the lids and ask the child to push the macaroni through the lid with the square or place four macaroni in the lid with the number "4" etc.

Children love to hear their shaking instrument after they have filled it with macaroni! This activity can also be done with other items such as pennies or beans.

Targeted Fine Motor Development:
- Pincer control
- Tripod grasp
- Intrinsic hand strengthening
- Hand separation
- Bimanual hand use
- Finger translation

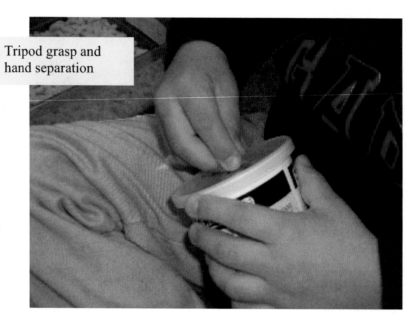

Tripod grasp and hand separation

Learning Goals:
- Measurement (fill a container)
- Description of qualities (describe how it sounds)
- Similarity and differences (penny vs. macaroni)
- Counting ("put 10 pieces in")
- One-to-one correspondence
- Shape/Letter recognition (draw shapes on lids of containers)

Suggested Positioning: The child should work on the floor.

MAGNA DOODLE

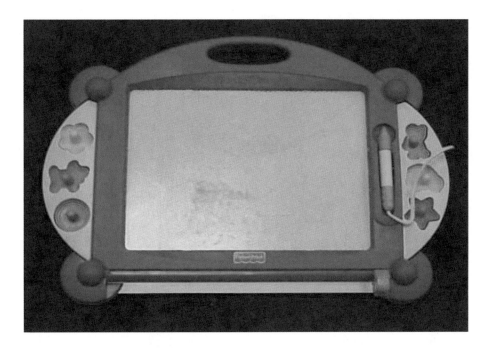

Description of Activity: The child draws and writes on magnetic Magna Doodle. The Magna Doodle is another unique surface for practicing drawing. Find as many different unique items for your child to write with, such as Aquadoodle, Glowdoodle, and so forth.

Targeted Fine Motor Development:
- Tripod Grasp
- Visual-motor development
- Visual perception
- Wrist extension
- Bilateral hand use (when erasing)
- Proximal stability
- Crossing midline (when erasing)

Learning Goals:
- Developmental strokes
- Shapes, letters, and numbers
- Holding a writing implement
- Left to right progression

Positioning: Place the Magna Doodle on a vertical surface to promote wrist extension and proximal stability.

NUTS 'N BOLTS

Description of Activity: The child matches up various-sized nuts and bolts and PVC piping, and screws them together.

Targeted Fine Motor Development:
- Manipulate small parts
- Distal finger control
- Pronation/Supination
- Proximal stability
- Finger translation

Learning Goals:
- Counting
- Matching
- Size and qualities (large/medium/small; long/short; light/heavy)
- Sorting (sort according size or length; nut or bolt, plastic or metal)
- Part to whole

Suggested Positioning: The child can either work on the floor or at a child-sized table.

PEGBOARD RESOURCE SET

Description of Activity: This pegboard set has small pegs that are challenging to hold and manipulate. Children can copy designs you make or those that are provided in the set. The following suggestions enhance this activity:

🖊 Have your child hold extra pegs in his dominant hand as they place pegs in the holes. Do not allow him to use his other hand to assist bringing pegs from the palm of his hand to fingertips (translation).

🖊 After the pegboard pattern is completed, children enjoy flipping it over and using their thumbs to punch the pegs out. The pegs fly across the room and it is a great motivator for completing the pegboard design.

Targeted Fine Motor Development:
- Hand separation (little finger and ring finger tucked under)
- Hand arch development/translation skills
- Tripod grasp
- Wrist extension
- Shoulder girdle and proximal stability
- Eye-hand coordination and visual-perception

Learning Goals:
- Shapes and colors
- Horizontal, vertical, diagonal lines, cross, and X
- Left to right progression
- Sequencing and patterning (red, yellow, blue, red, yellow, blue)
- Orientation (top, bottom, middle, above, below)
- Size (small circle/large circle)
- Counting; one-to-one correlation
- First and last; more/less
- Numbers and letters

Suggested Positioning: Place the pegboard on the floor or on a vertical surface to promote wrist extension.

         www.handylearning.com

LACING CARDS

Description of Activity: The child laces these cards and in doing so completes a picture. The child must lace in the proper sequence. **Drawing dotted lines on the back of the cards to cue where to lace is helpful.** Some cards are more difficult than others. Numbering the cards according to difficulty level may help to appropriately select difficulty levels.

Targeted Fine Motor Development:
- Manipulate small objects
- Bilateral integration
- Sequencing/Motor planning
- Pincer grasp
- Finger translation

Learning Goals:
- Sequencing
- Colors (laces are different colors)
- Orientation (above, below, on top, underneath)
- Visual perception/Visual closure

Suggested Positioning: The child should work on the floor or at a child-sized table. Pull the child's chair slightly away from the table to prevent leaning on the table for stabilization. Make sure the child approaches the task with palms slightly turned up (supinated) and not pronated. See photo below.

PLAY-DOH FUN

Description of Activity: Play-Doh is a relatively common item that offers many benefits. The child can engage in a variety of activities with playdoh including:

- Roll Play-Doh into small little balls with the fingertips
- Roll into large balls with palms of hands and fingers straight
- Roll into snakes and cut into pieces with plastic knife
- Make thumbprints in the snake by squeezing it between thumb and index, thumb and middle finger, thumb and fourth finger, etc.
- Construct simple 3-D designs like snowmen
- Make spaghetti with press and cut with scissors or knife
- Make "pancakes" with palms of hands and use cookie cutters to cut out shapes
- Use pattern rolling pins to flatten putty
- Cut flattened putty into halves/quarters with plastic knife or rolling knife
- Use Dough Stampers to make imprints (make sure they hold these with their fingers, NOT a fisted grasp)
- Poke holes with dull pencil and have child trace dot to dot through the Play-Doh with dull pencil
- Cut Play-Doh with scissors. Cut along lines and/or shapes drawn in Play-Doh with dull pencil

Targeted Fine Motor Development: *(on next page)*

Learning Goals: *(on next page)*

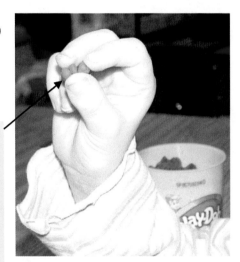

By rolling small balls at the fingertips, this child is developing in-hand manipulation skills such as translation.

She is developing hand arches and intrinsic hand muscles.

PLAY-DOH, continued

Targeted Fine Motor Development:
- Tripod grasp (with Dough Stampers and dull pencil)
- Cutting Skills
- Bilateral integration (cutting with plastic knife and scissors)
- Intrinsic hand muscle development
- Proprioceptive (making pancakes) and Tactile sensory input
- Visual-motor (drawing shapes/connecting dots in Play-Doh)

Learning Goals:
- Shapes
- Developmental strokes
- Cutting skills
- Constructional tasks (building snowman)
- Left to right progression (making dots with dull pencil, drawing)

Cutting Play-Doh with a knife develops hand arches.

Dough Stampers—have your child use a tripod grasp.

Thumb opposition.

Cutting Play-Doh is an excellent way to first learn how to cut.

SQUIGGLE PEN

Description of Activity: The child uses a pen that vibrates to draw and write. The vibration offers unique feedback to the child and is fun to use. Vibration may be an effective way to learn kinesthetically where other methods may have not been successful.

Targeted Fine Motor Development:
- Tripod grasp
- Writing skills
- Visual-motor skills

Learning Goals:
- Writing and prewriting
- Developmental strokes
- Shapes, letters, and numbers
- Holding a writing implement

Suggested Positioning: The child can be prone on the floor, standing at a vertical surface, or writing at the table. They should hold the pen with the thumb, index, and middle finger if possible. However, this pen is large and cumbersome for most children so do not worry if they use a different grasp than what they use when holding a crayon.

STAMPS

Description of Activity: The child uses a small stamp and stamps within a given parameter on a page, i.e., maze, shape.

Targeted Fine Motor Development:
- Tripod grasp
- Hand arches/hand separation
- Crossing midline
- Eye-hand coordination

Learning Goals:
- Left to right progression
- Sequencing
- Counting (place 10 stamps on the line)
- Orientation (place the stamps in the middle of the circle, outside the circle, above, below, etc.)
- Visual-motor skills
- Shapes (stamping inside or around the circle, the square, the triangle, etc.)

Suggested Positioning: The child should hold the stamp with their first three fingers, NOT a whole fisted grasp. Set the stamp pad up so that it encourages the child to reach across the middle of their body. The stamping paper can be placed on a vertical surface or an inclined surface such as a 3" three-ring binder to encourage wrist extension and stabilization.

Wrist is not in extension.

A better setup is to place the paper on an easel to provide a vertical

This child is stabilizing his trunk against the table.

STENCILS

Description of Activity: The child traces inside these stencils. The child can also finger-paint inside these stencils. The stencils should be taped firmly to a vertical surface such as a dry-erase board, chalkboard, or hung butcher paper.

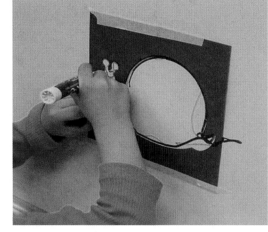

Targeted Fine Motor Development:
- Tripod grasp
- Wrist extension
- Proximal stability
- Eye-hand coordination
- Visual perception
- Crossing midline

Learning Goals:
- Size and shape (especially when coupled with smaller stencils)
- Colors

Suggested Positioning: Children should work on the floor or on a vertical surface such as an easel or dry-erase board.

STEREOGNOSIS BOX

Description of Activity: A hole is cut out in the side of a shoe box for the child's hand. Cover the hole with a washcloth so the child cannot peek. Place several items in the box for the child to find: button, paperclip, small eraser, small pom-pom, animal counters, shapes, plastic numbers/letters, etc. Items no larger than one inch are best. Have duplicate items for visual reference. Ask the child to find a particular item by feel alone.

A fun alternative to making your own is **<u>What's in Ned's Head</u>,** a game that can be purchased at any toy department.

Targeted Fine Motor Development:
- Tactile discrimination (imperative for learning)
- Hand translation skills
- Visual perception (by visually confirming once item is found)

Learning Goals:
- Understanding qualities of size, shape, and texture
- Learning shapes (circle, square, triangle, etc. Use Feel 'n Find puzzle pieces)
- Describing attributes/similarities and differences
- Sequencing (find the button THEN the paperclip)
- One-to-one correspondence/counting
- Grouping/sorting (put all the soft things together)
- Matching
- Seriation (ordering items according to size, e.g. smallest to largest)
- Orientation (place the button ON TOP of the paperclip)

Suggested Positioning: The child can be either seated at a table or on the floor.

STRAW CONNECTORS
(Brilliant Builders)

Description of Activity: The child assembles straws with connector joints and forms different structures and shapes. Cut the straws to different lengths to provide a wide variety of building possibilities. With shorter straws, children can even form shapes such as circles and octagons. Encourage the child to form three-dimensional shapes. Children can also form some letters. NOTE: these are now called "**Brilliant Builders.**"

Targeted Fine Motor Development:
- Wrist extension
- Separation of the hand
- Proximal stabilization at the trunk and shoulder
- Visual-perceptual skills

Learning Goals:
- Shapes
- Colors
- Patterning
- Letter formation
- Size and quantity (how long, how tall, how wide, etc.)

Suggested Positioning: The child should work on the floor and away from external support surfaces.

STRINGING BEADS

Description of Activity: The child strings small ¼" wooden beads of different shapes and colors. The child should manipulate the string with their dominant hand and hold the bead with their nondominant hand.

Targeted Fine Motor Development:
- Thumb opposition
- Separation of the hand
- Distal control of the fingers
- Intrinsic muscle development
- Finger translation

Learning Goals
- Shapes
- Colors
- Patterning/Sequencing
- Counting/Math concepts

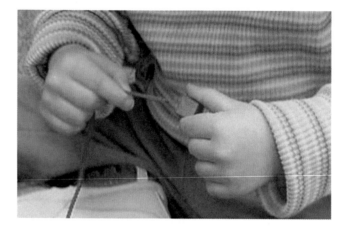

Suggested Positioning: The child can sit on the floor for this activity. Do not allow the child to stabilize their arms on a table or to push their elbows into their sides for stabilization. Elbows should be a couple of inches away from the trunk and stabilization should occur at the shoulders. The child should be holding the beads with their fingertips.

TABLETOP EASEL

Description of Activity: Children can color, write, draw, and paint on this easel. **The vertical surface is important for hand development and prewriting skills**. The easel has a dry-erase board and a chalkboard. A clip can be used at the top to hold paper for coloring or painting. Wikki Stix stick on the dry-erase board side (see Activity: Wikki Stix). The chalkboard side is preferred for drawing and writing as it gives more feedback and control than the dry-erase side.

Targeted Fine Motor Development:
- Wrist extension
- Separation of the hand
- Proximal stabilization at the trunk and shoulder
- Visual-motor skills

Learning Goals:
- Shapes
- Colors
- Patterning
- Developmental strokes
- Letter formation

Suggested Positioning: Working on a vertical surface is critical to proper hand development. It places the wrist in extension, which is the position of function for the hand. In addition, it builds the stabilizing muscles of the shoulder and trunk that allow for fluid movement at the fingertips. The child may either stand or sit to work at the easel.

TACTILE BINS

Description of Activity: Children place hands in birdseed/rice for tactile stimulation and exploration. Powder their hands with baby powder to keep birdseed from sticking to their hands.

Allow them to pour, sift, bury, and find items. Place shapes, magnet letters, numbers, animals, and any other educationally related item in the birdseed for them to find. Use small containers for pouring such as film containers. Plastic bottles with screw lids are fun for filling up and pouring out.

To develop hand arches, have the child hold as much rice or birdseed as they can by cupping it in one hand. Then have the child grip the birdseed in the hand and let it "rain" out the pinky side of the hand (see photo).

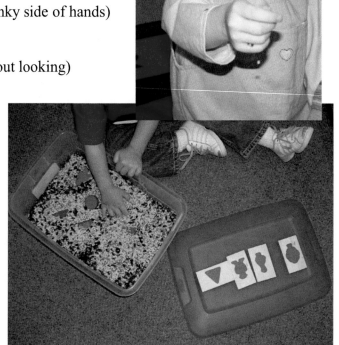

Targeted Fine Motor Development:
- Tactile Discrimination
- Hand arches (by pouring birdseed out pinky side of hands)
- Pronation/Supination (pouring)
- Sensory modulation/input
- Stereognosis (finding hidden items without looking)
- Hand translation

Learning Goals:
- Explore a variety of tactile media
- Letters and numbers
- Pouring
- Measurement
- Size and quantity (small bottle vs. larger bottle)
- Matching
- Grouping/Sorting

Suggested Positioning: Children should be on the floor. A drop cloth is recommended.

TONGS

Description of Activity: Tongs develop the small muscles of the hands and the hand arches. Using tongs also teaches the child to coordinate timing and sequencing. They are also considered a pre-scissor activity.

Tongs should be used on a daily basis as an integral part of your child's activities where possible. The child can use tongs to sort, clean up his room, count, glue small items (such as macaroni or hole-punched shapes) on paper. Using tongs of different sizes and resistance are of added benefit.

Make sure the tongs are positioned correctly in the child's hands. See "Suggested Positioning" on next page.

Ideas:
- In addition to Pom-poms and erasers, use educationally related items such as small eraser numbers or letters, animals for sorting, etc.
- Write numbers inside plastic bowls and ask the child to put the correct amount of items in each bowl.
- Do the same with letters and have the child sort items according to first letters.
- Have "Tong Races": The child holds an item in their tongs and places it in the appropriate container across the room. This encourages prolonged resistance.

Targeted Fine Motor Development: *(on next page)*

Learning Goals: *(on next page)*

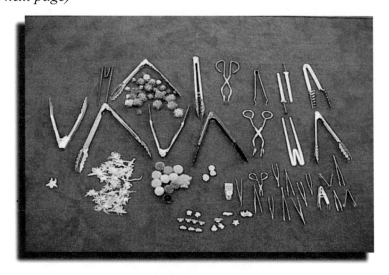

Tongs to Tweezers

TONGS, continued

fa

Targeted Fine Motor Development:
- Hand separation; arches
- Intrinsic hand muscle development
- Thumb opposition
- Motor sequencing
- Eye-hand coordination

Learning Goals:
- Sorting
- Counting
- Matching
- Letter and number recognition
- Spelling of name, etc.
- Patterning and sequencing (line up items by color)
- Orientation concepts (place it IN, ON, BEHIND, etc.)

The hand goes on top as pictured. Fingers control the tongs. The tongs are away from the palm of the hand.

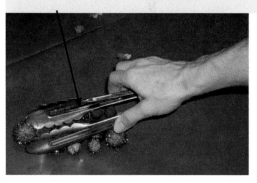

Suggested Positioning: Tongs should be positioned in the hands so that the child uses his fingertips to squeeze the tongs. The tongs should not touch the palm of the hand. The hand should be on **top** of the tongs, not underneath. Tong activity is best done on the floor to promote trunk stability and wrist extension.

Strawberry Huller

Picklers: syringe-like spring-loaded grabbers!

Great for building thumb muscles.

TOOTHPICKS AND STYROFOAM

Description of Activity: The child pushes colored toothpicks into a Styrofoam sheet. A shape, letter, or pattern is provided. The pattern may be on a piece of paper for them to replicate or you can have them put the toothpicks directly through the paper by attaching the paper to the Styrofoam.

Targeted Fine Motor Development:
- Hand separation (little finger and ring finger tucked under)
- Hand arch development
- Tripod grasp
- Wrist extension
- Shoulder girdle and proximal stability
- Eye-hand coordination and visual perception

Learning Goals:
- Shapes and colors
- Horizontal, vertical, and diagonal lines
- Left to right progression
- Sequencing and patterning (red, yellow, blue, red, yellow, blue)
- Orientation (top, bottom, middle, above, below)
- Size (small circle/large circle)
- Counting; one-to-one correlation
- First and last, more/less
- Numbers and letters

Suggested Positioning:
Place the Styrofoam vertically in back of chair. Have the child kneel in front of the chair and reach across chair seat to put toothpicks in. If the child can manage, do not allow them to stabilize their trunk on the chair.

WATER PLAY

Description of Activity: The child uses eye droppers, sponges, small basters, squirt bottles, squeeze toys, plastic syringes, and washcloths, to transfer water from one bin to another. Food coloring may be added to the water for additional fun. This is just plain fun and it builds hand muscles too!

Targeted Fine Motor Development:
- Thumb opposition
- Hand arches
- Pronation/Supination
- Intrinsic muscle development
- Pouring

Learning Goals:
- Concepts of measurement
- Size and quantity

Suggested Positioning: This is a tabletop activity. Towels for quick clean up are recommended.

WIKKI STIX

Description of Activity: Provide sample shapes, lines, numbers, or letters for children to replicate with their Wikki Stix. They can either copy it with their Wikki Stix, or place the Wikki Stix directly on a drawn sample.

Wikki Stix can be used to replicate shapes, letters, numbers, and lines. The also can be used to teach children to color and/or cut in between lines by offering kinesthetic feedback. They can be used to make mazes for children to draw or cut through.

They stick to most anything and are reusable!

Targeted Fine Motor Development:
- Eye-hand coordination
- Visual perception
- Distal use of fingers
- Hand arches
- Hand separation
- Wrist extension and proximal stability

Learning Goals:
- Shapes, Letters, Numbers
- Orientation (place yours above mine, beside mine, etc.)

Suggested Positioning: Use a vertical surface. The child can be either sitting or standing. Wikki Stix work well on a dry-erase board.

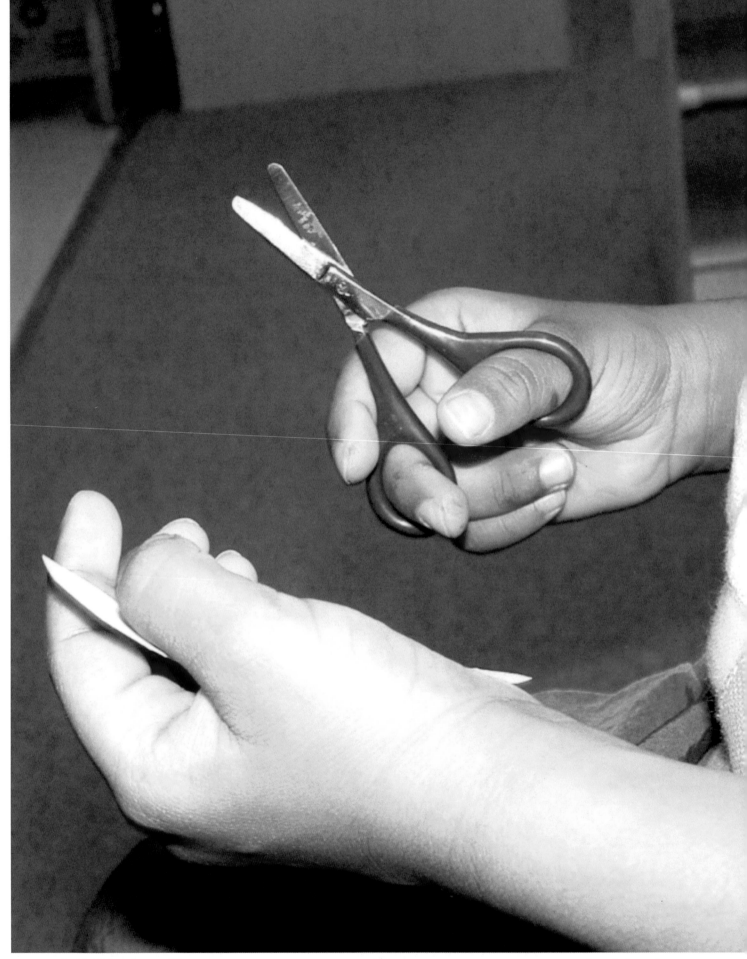

Teaching Cutting Skills

Two things can best facilitate helping a child to learn to cut with scissors: controlling the media that the child is cutting and positioning the child and the scissors appropriately.

It is important that the child assumes the correct hand, forearm, and trunk position during cutting. In addition, the child should have immediate success when cutting so to encourage a continued interest in the task.

Cutting Media:

As the environmental designer for the child, you can ensure success by thoughtfully planning what media the child is going to cut. Generally, the stiffer and smaller the media, the more immediate success your child will have.

An excellent media choice for the first attempts at cutting is straws. Straws are easy to control and require only one snip. By cutting straws the child will have success while learning the motor sequence of opening and closing the scissors.

For added fun, the straws tend to fly through the air in which the child takes great delight. After cutting the straws, the child can pick the straw cuttings up and string them with yarn to make a necklace.

After practice with the straws, draw marks on the straws for the child to cut on. This will prepare the child for cutting along a line and gives him the opportunity to practice lining up his scissors with a visual reference.

Once the child has demonstrated success with the straws, change the media to a slightly larger and thinner material: index cards. Start by using small blank index cards. Then move to drawing straight lines across the index cards, then curved lines, and finally draw shapes on the index card for the child to cut out. Once this is mastered, move up to the large index cards, then half sheets of regular paper, and finally to full sheets of paper.

By controlling the media, you are grading the activity for success. Being an environmental designer for the child is a powerful implementation tool.

Positioning While Cutting:

Trunk

It is best to have the child sit in a chair while cutting. Make sure his feet are touching the floor and he can sit up against the chair back. This offers him plenty of external stability for the fine motor task of cutting.

The child will learn cutting more quickly if he is pulled away from the table. This way, he will not have the table to lean on for external support and will be free to hold his paper or cutting media without obstruction. He can hold the cutting media at the height that works best for him. Also, by pulling him away from the table you will be designing the environment so that he will have to exercise his proximal stabilizing muscles in his trunk and shoulders.

Forearms and Hands

When first learning to cut, the child will most likely approach the task with a pronated, or palms down, position. He may even try to cut from the top of the media in toward himself. To remedy this, simply sit behind him and lightly reposition his forearms so that he is in a more supinated position. (See photo C1). His assist hand (nondominant hand) should be holding the media with the palm facing toward the ceiling. His cutting hand should have the thumb on top and elbow toward his body instead of pointing away from his body (See photo C2).

His cutting hand should hold the scissors with the thumb and middle finger in the loop. The index finger should **not** be in the loop. The stabilizing side of his hand, the Secret Side, should be curled into his palm for hand separation (See photo C2).

By using these approaches for teaching cutting, the child will have quick success in learning the skill of cutting!

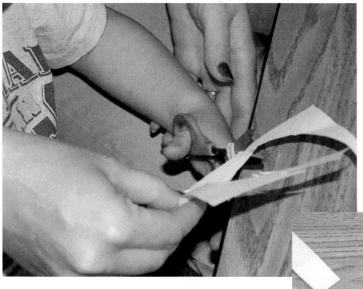

Photo C1 – repositioning for supination

Photo C2—Hand separation; pinky in palm

His index finger is not positioned properly and should be outside of the loop.

The student is working away from the table to promote proximal stability.

 www.handylearning.com

Cutting Kit

Taking the time to assemble a Cutting Kit will encourage frequent and successful cutting practice. When it is time to practice cutting, all you have to do is pull out a plastic bin and all of your supplies are in one place. The Cutting Kit activity page describes how to assemble a cutting kit with a variety of media.

Description of Activity: The child cuts various media according to skill level to develop cutting skills. Media is roughly graded from easiest to most difficult as follows. Lines can be added to any of the media to increase visual-motor skills.

- Cutting straws
- Snipping Play-Doh
- Snipping index cards
- Cutting across small index cards
- Cutting across large index cards
- Cutting half page of card stock
- Snipping strips (1–2" wide) of regular paper
- Cutting across half page of regular paper
- Cutting regular paper

Generally, the thicker and the smaller the media, the easier it is for the child to cut. Benbow scissors are highly recommended to encourage proper hand placement during cutting. See Resources in the Appendix to acquire these scissors.

To assemble a Cutting Kit, include the following in a plastic bin:
- All of the above listed cutting media
- A black marker to draw lines on the media
- An assortment of scissors to promote interest and variety

If set up properly, cutting is an inherent activity for promoting hand separation.

www.handylearning.com

Getting a Grip

Although there is an optimal way to hold a pencil while writing—the tripod grasp—it is not the only way to hold a pencil. In fact, how a pencil is held is not necessarily a predictor of handwriting legibility. **As long as the intrinsic muscles are well developed and involved during the act of handwriting, the writing should be legible. Intrinsic muscle development is the key.**

If the child has engaged in Handy Learning and other fine motor activities, chances are he will be developmentally ready to hold the pencil and will do so correctly without the need for instruction. However, if the hands are underdeveloped or the child is pushed too early, a less efficient pencil grasp may result. In that instance, it might be prudent to take the pencil away and do some more Handy Learning activities.

The following are several pencil grasps and their efficiency levels.

A note on the Adapted Tripod Grasp:

The adapted tripod grasp is perfectly suitable for handwriting and offers inherent stability by placing the pencil between the index and middle finger. Drafters were once taught to use this grasp because they required a high degree of control over their pencil.

The adapted tripod grasp is particularly useful if your child has lax finger joints or is what you might call "double jointed." This grasp is also recommended for persons with arthritis as it alleviates the stress on the thumb joints. If you are looking for a quick fix to increase your child's pencil control, the adapted tripod grasp may be the answer.

The following pictures and descriptions are adapted from Mary Benbow, OTR "Efficient and Non-efficient Pencil Grasps."

Acceptable Pencil Grasps

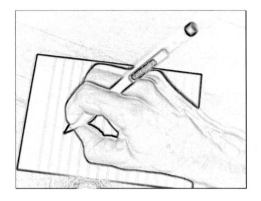

Tripod Grasp

Adapted Tripod Grasp

Less Acceptable Pencil Grasps

Thumb Wrap Grasp

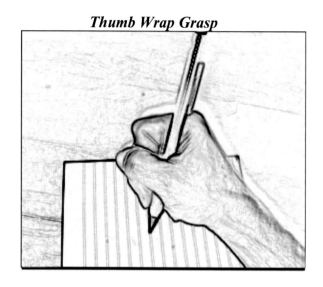

Lateral Hook Grasp

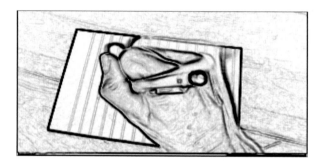

Index Hook Grasp

Primitive Pencil Grasps

Palmar Grasp

Pronated Grasp

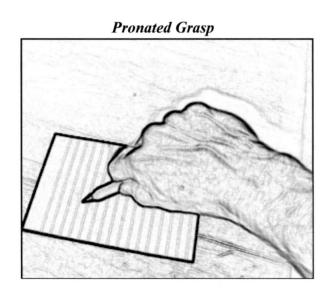

Grasp pattern descriptions adapted from Mary Benbow, OTR

Special Section: Handwriting Issues for Occupational Therapists

The bulk of referrals for school-based Occupational Therapy services are for poor or illegible handwriting. The expectation from teachers, parents, and administrators is that most handwriting issues fall within our service domain and are appropriate for Occupational Therapy intervention. However, many handwriting issues may stem from other, non-Occupational Therapy related problems. It is important that we are able to differentiate these problems while at the same time place appropriate students on Occupational Therapy services.

Occupational Therapists should be able to:

1. Recognize poor handwriting
2. Properly evaluate and identify the etiology behind the poor handwriting
3. Make appropriate Occupational Therapy service decisions for students
4. Be able to communicate clearly to the parents, teachers, and administrators what the probable issues are and how they can best be addressed

Handwriting Evaluation Test:

The following exercise is designed to help hone these skills.

This exercise is designed to be a learning experience by defining clear-cut symptoms and clues. However, as always, a full evaluation of a student should be completed and all aspects should be examined and considered. Therefore, please keep in mind that this is a LEARNING experience and not a formula for determining eligibility for Occupational Therapy services!

After years of scrutinizing handwriting samples from students of different ages, abilities, and disabilities, certain patterns became evident. While not absolute, handwriting samples often reveal patterns that relate to a diagnosis. Recognizing these patterns can offer the Occupational Therapist hints and clues as to whether the student should be placed on service for handwriting and what aspects should and should not be targeted in service delivery.

As a side note, if you are struggling with the credibility of this exercise, allow me to share that I had a group of experienced teachers attempt this exercise. They correctly matched all the samples within ten minutes!

Over the course of their long careers, they had seen far more handwriting samples than Occupational Therapists see. Because they had observed volumes of handwriting samples, these teachers were well practiced and thus able to recognize the patterns with ease.

They scored a 100%! Each received a smiley face on their paper for such an excellent score!

You will be given six handwriting samples on the next few pages. Try to match the six diagnoses to the appropriate handwriting sample.

Handwriting Sample (Student A–F)   ## Diagnosis

_____   ADHD

_____   Emotionally Disabled

_____   Fine Motor (mild CP)

_____   Learning Disability

_____   Emotionally Disabled

_____   ADHD

Student A

Note: *The teacher wrote: "I want a white January again." The student then copied it.*

Spelling Homework
January 16, 2007

Write each word three (3) times.

January	January	January	January
white	White	White	White
who	who	Who	Who
win	Win	win	Win
with	with	with	With
want	Want	Want	Want
went	went	We nt	went
after	after	after	after
again	again	again	again
any	any	any	any
as	as	as	as
ask	ask	ask	ask

Write a sentence using at least 2 spelling words.

I want a white January again.

I want a white January again

Note: *The student dictated the sentence: "I drew a stick of butter." The teacher wrote it down and then the student copied the sentence.*

date 1-18-2007

Idrewastikofbut

I drew a stick of butter.

Super Job

BEFORE   4th grade   Dylan
                                                     3/23/04

On Spring Brick I

want to to o k) ho

I rode some goats in a farm where
                                   my aunt
I food baby goats with a bottle.   lives.

I food babey gots

3 Went fshing yond

We went fishing and did not catch anything.

went to tone tof
Sno warrer

wnewh to

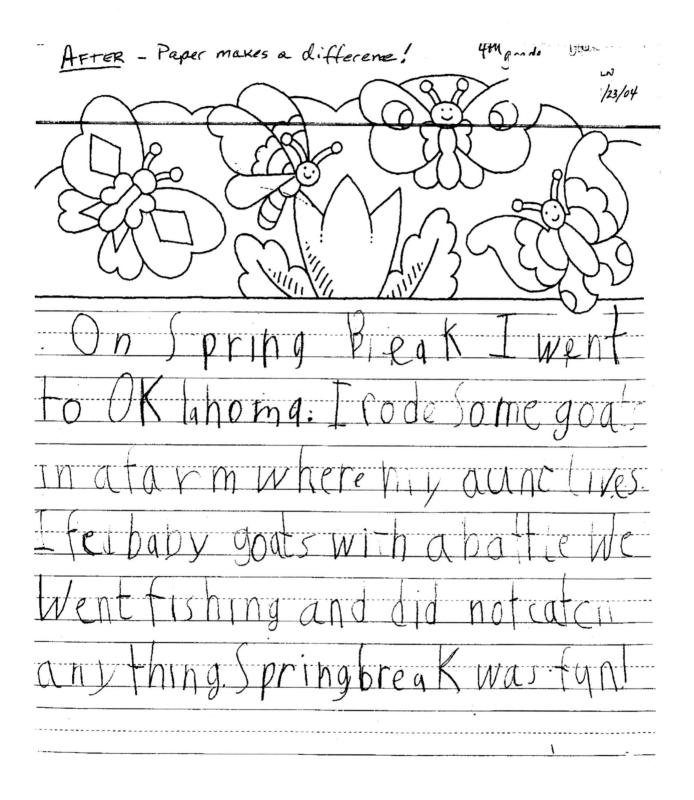

AFTER - Paper makes a difference!   4th grade

1/23/04

On Spring Break I went
to OKlahoma. I rode some goats
in a farm where my aunt lives.
I fed baby goats with a battle. We
Went fishing and did not catch
any thing. Spring break was fun!

         www.handylearning.com

Student C

Note: The words "win," "with," after," "again" were written by the teacher.

1. January 4/12
   Student Teacher
2. w white
3. who
4. w win
5. w with
6. a after
7. a again
8. any
9. as
10. a ask

11. wfot want
12. wlet went

Spelling Homework
January 16, 2007

Write each word three (3) times.

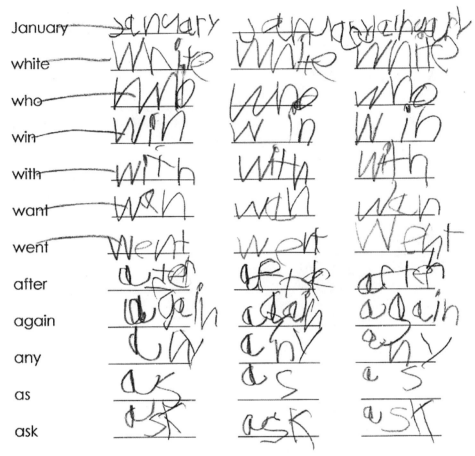

January	January	January	January
white	white	white	white
who	who	who	who
win	win	win	win
with	with	with	with
want	want	want	want
went	went	went	went
after	after	after	after
again	again	again	again
any	any	any	any
as	as	as	as
ask	ask	ask	ask

Write a sentence using at least 2 spelling words.

nh

94

1. January
2. ~~White~~ white   7/12
3. who
4. wih
5. with
6. ~~after~~ after
7. a gg n again
8. any
9. as
10. ~~task~~

11. ~~Want~~ want
12. ~~Wet~~ went

White

after

again

want

went

Spelling Homework
January 18, 2007

Write the words 2 times each.

make	~~make~~	make
me	me	me
my	~~my~~	~~my~~
not	not	hot
one	one	one
January	danuary	January

Student F

Note: *The dark print is the teacher sample. The student took a minimum of 45 minutes to complete this assignment.*

NAME _Wow_

Ryan said, "Who are you?"

Ryan said, "Who are you?"

Ryan said, "I like school."

Ryan said, "I like school."

Ryan said, "Look out!"

Ryan said, "Look out!"

Ryan said, "Go get it."

Ryan said, "Go get it."

Note: *The student wrote the word "Wow" and drew the stars. He was to put a check mark next to his answer.*

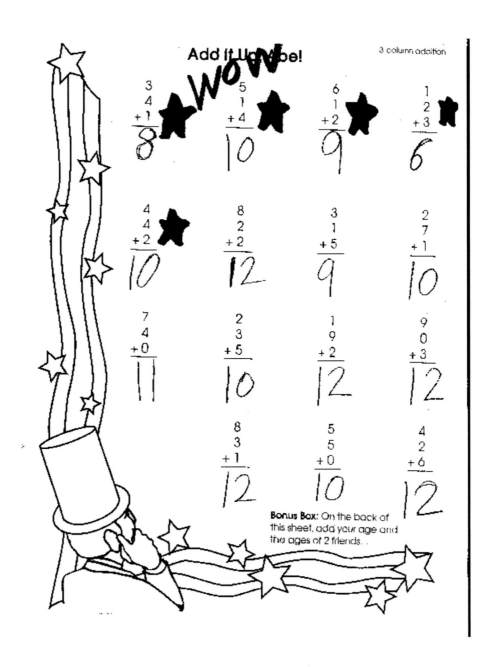

Answers:

<u>Handwriting Sample (Student A—F)</u>   <u>Diagnosis</u>

Student A   Learning Disability

Student B   ADHD

Student C   Emotionally Disturbed

Student D   ADHD

Student E   Fine Motor (mild CP)

Student F   Emotionally Disturbed

The Why's Behind the Answers

Student A:

Student A has a <u>Learning Disability</u>. Learning disabilities often become evident when a student must multilayer information or multitask. For instance, a student with a learning disability might be able to copy letters of the alphabet successfully. However, if asked to write them down from memory in alphabetical order, they may falter because they must:
a.) remember the letters in order
b.) remember what the letter looks like
c.) put the letter down on paper

If a student with a learning disability is asked to draw a picture and write a sentence about it, this will be even more challenging. The student must formulate an idea in their head, hold the memory of the idea, draw the idea on paper from scratch, then create a sentence by writing individual letter formations, form whole words, remember to capitalize at the beginning of the sentence, punctuate at the end of the sentence AND get the spelling right! To a student with a learning disability, this can be extremely daunting. Student A had such an assignment.

Here is how you can tell **Student A** has a <u>Learning Disability</u>:

Letter Formations:

Look at **Student A**'s letters out of context. Put your fingers on either side of letters randomly to isolate them and determine whether you can read the letter out of context. When isolating and looking at the letters out of context, **Student A** demonstrates legible letter formations. Her letters are overall legible and consistently formed.

Drawing:

Student A drew a stick of butter. This student simplified the task for herself by drawing what she could, then naming it after she drew it. Most students approach this task the other way around. First they think of something they want to draw, ("I'll draw a house"), and then they attempt to draw it.

Writing the Sentence:

Student A dictated the sentence to the teacher and the teacher wrote the sentence for her to copy. This helps to break down the task and minimize the multilayered demands. However, she misspelled words even when copying from same-plane, near-point. Spelling errors are common with children with LD even when copying.

Conclusion: Because this student demonstrates the ability to form letters legibly, she demonstrates the foundational skills of visual-motor and fine motor control for handwriting. Her handwriting issues therefore do not necessarily stem from Occupational Therapy related concerns.

Instead, her handwriting deteriorates when multilayered demands are placed on her. This is directly related to her learning disability. Therefore, she may not be appropriate for OT service (unless of course she had other school functional delays related to sensory processing, self-care, etc.).

This student's handwriting issues are better addressed by the special education teacher who is trained to modify toward the student's learning needs.

Student B:

Student B has <u>ADHD</u>. Individuals with ADHD have difficulties focusing and attending appropriately. They also struggle with organizing themselves in space. This lack of organization is pervasive. The individual may have difficulties organizing personal space, workspace and even organizing on the writing page.

The key clue to **Student B**'s handwriting sample is that there is a BEFORE and AFTER (this, by the way, was not before and after medication)! When the student was given clear visual parameters to write within, his handwriting markedly improved. Providing clean, clear visual parameters for students with ADHD is a highly effective strategy for improving handwriting and messy work papers. Clearly lined paper with simple black-and-white lines, highlighted notebook paper, or even boxes drawn for individual words, are all good strategies for providing clear visual parameters.

Here are further clues regarding **Student B** and ADHD:

- Scratch-outs rather than erasures. Students with ADHD rarely take the time to fully erase. They scratch out instead because it is quicker.

- Inconsistent letter formations. Look at the letter "a" in the first sentence. Virtually every time the student writes this letter, he does so in a different way. Letter formations of students with ADHD are *consistently inconsistent*.

Conclusion: This student obviously can form letters appropriately and can produce legible handwriting. Thus the student demonstrates foundational skills related to handwriting. This student is a good candidate for consult services in order to provide strategies for the classroom teacher and student with an emphasis on providing visual parameters and organizational techniques. It would also be recommended that this student begin developing keyboarding (computer) skills for later grades.

Student C:

Student C is a student with <u>Emotional Disability</u>. One way to identify students with emotional concerns is to observe how they express themselves on paper. This student has expended a tremendous amount of energy on something extraneous to the task.

Look at the lines on the right-hand side of the paper. This student scribbled each individual writing line, left to right. After taking the time to complete that, the student drew a curvy line right down the middle. Finally, the student drew a rectangle around the entire area, as if to frame the effort.

These efforts were time consuming, and required energy and focus on something other than the assignment. This student is engaging in extraneous expressions. Extraneous expressions are any scribbles, drawings, and written output that consume a considerable amount of energy but that do not fit into the assignment or time allotment. These types of extraneous expressions are usually out of context and somewhat difficult to understand when reviewing the handwriting sample. When one looks at the page, one wonders, "What happened here?"

In general, however, if you look at this student's letter formations out of context, they are legible and consistent. The overall messy appearance to the page has little to do with handwriting or fine motor ability.

Conclusion: This student probably would not be a good candidate for school-based Occupational Therapy service for handwriting.

Student D:

Student D has <u>ADHD</u>. His letter formations are inconsistent. Look at the letter "g" in the word "again" on his first page. Each time the student writes this letter, it is approached differently in size, stroke and appearance.

Now look at the word "again" on the second page of this student's handwriting sample. You can see that with good visual parameters, the student demonstrates better letter formations, improved legibility, and overall improved organization on the page.

Conclusion: This student received consult Occupational Therapy services to help to set up his environment for improved organization and handwriting legibility. He did not receive direct, pull-out service to work specifically on handwriting or letter formations. He received daily practice in the Resource classroom using the Handwriting Without Tears program (www.hwtears.com) which was implemented for the entire class and carried through by the teacher.

Side note: This student's handwriting sample is an assignment to practice writing his spelling words three times in a row. For most students in special education, this is rarely an effective teaching strategy. This type of assignment only encourages the student to repeat his own mistakes, both with letter formations and spelling!

Student E:

Student E has mild <u>Cerebral Palsy</u> with resulting <u>fine motor delay</u>. You can tell that he does not have ADHD because his letter formations are fairly consistent. True to a fine motor control issue, he is able to improve with repetition. In this instance, the assignment of repeating the words is effective. In addition, note that he spells each word correctly, thus demonstrating the ability to multilayer demands. This student does have a shortened assignment due to motor fatigue.

Conclusion: This student is certainly appropriate for Occupational Therapy service!

Side Note: This student is now in second grade and has beautiful handwriting. He received direct OT service in the classroom setting. Intervention included the Handy Learning activities and using Herbi Writer (www.herbi.org) to learn and practice proper letter formations. Both Handy Learning and Herbi Writer were done with the entire Resource classroom as an integrative model to providing service. Not only did this student benefit from the intervention, so did all the students in his classroom.

Student F:

Student F has an <u>Emotional Disability</u> specific to <u>Obsessive Compulsive Disorder</u>. In the first page of this student's handwriting sample, the student is attempting to perfectly replicate the sample. The student traces back over letters and attempts to make the letters intricately aligned and matched to the sample. The fact that it took the student forty-five minutes to complete the assignment was not due to lack of fine motor control, but due to his perseverance on perfection.

In the second sample, the student was to put a check beside the correct answers. However, the student preferred to draw stars instead. Each star is nearly identical and each star reportedly took the student about two minutes to draw, thus making the student fall behind in his other daily assignments.

Conclusion: Although Occupational Therapists are trained in the mental health field, the school system rarely uses OT in this capacity. This student might benefit from Occupational Therapy services to learn anxiety-reducing strategies, but it would be difficult to convince the IEP team to allow for this type of OT service. Certainly working on handwriting would not be warranted as this student clearly demonstrates the visual motor and fine motor prerequisites for letter formation and the student does produce legible handwriting.

Side note: On a one-time consult, I offered this student a mechanical pencil and talked to him about practicing "imperfection." I explained to the student that the pencil would help reduce his pencil pressure and would never need sharpening, thus it would provide a consistent writing lead. The student was highly intelligent and immediately took to the pencil. He said, "This pencil will help me when I need to move on to the next letter." He dubbed it his "moving-on pencil." I was delighted, and so was he. (He then proceeded to tell me that he needed two mechanical pencils . . . because everyone should always have a backup pencil)!

Handwriting Issues Conclusion

There are many reasons for poor or illegible handwriting. Many of these reasons are not necessarily related to foundational skills that Occupational Therapy addresses. If the handwriting delay is due to poor visual-motor skill, poor fine motor control or even poor sensory processing and modulation, than it is certainly appropriate to initiate Occupational Therapy services.

If however, the student demonstrates good letter formations out of context, and can form individual letters appropriately, then the "messy" handwriting is more likely due to other, non-Occupational Therapy related issues. These students (of which there are many), are best served by other professionals such as the special education teacher.

Appendix

Troubleshooting Ideas

If the student has difficulty with:

Organizing written work on a page

Try this:

Offer visual parameters such as:

- Highlighted lines
- Boxes for single-word answers
- Special paper (Every other line highlighted. This is available in office supply stores).
- Graph paper for organizing math problems
- A dark or highlighted line down the left margin to keep left alignment
- Fold notebook paper in half lengthwise for spelling test and lists- prenumber the lines.

Producing legible handwritten work

Try this:

- Allow for keyboarding/typing on computer
- Use adapted paper as above
- Use a mechanical pencil
- Skip lines on paper
- Have the student write smaller (smaller= better control and decreased impulsivity)
- Isolate and remediate the letters that are not formed correctly (usually only a few letters formed incorrectly make handwriting illegible)

Handwriting is too dark or light

Try this:

- Put any of the following under the paper for more feedback: small stack of paper, book, light sandpaper, Dycem (nonslip rubber mat)
- Have the student squeeze a squeeze ball in the nondominant hand while writing
- Offer tactile experience before writing to "wake up" the hand (playing in sand, birdseed, rice, shaving cream)
- Have the student weight bear (place weight through) their arms and hands while standing at the desk prior to handwriting
- Put weights such as small nuts and bolts on the pencil for increased feedback

Poor spacing between words, impulsive during writing

Try this:

- Have the student write in cursive
- If manuscript, have the student underline each word as he finishes the word
- Teach the student to exaggerate the space
- Use popsicle sticks or finger to space between words

Letter reversals

Try this:

- Make an index card with the most often reversed letters (b, d and z) printed on the right edge for a visual reference
- Have an alphabet strip on the student's desk

Poor fine motor control

Try this:

- Utilize Handy Learning activities
- Visit LISD OT website (www.lisd.net) follow links: Departments, Special Education, Support and Services, Occupational Therapy, Fine Motor Skills

Sensory processing

Try this:

- Visit LISD OT website (www.lisd.net) follow links: Departments, Special Education, Support and Services, Occupational Therapy, for information and strategies for Sensory Processing.
- Look at:
  - What is Sensory Processing
  - Sensory Activities
  - What is a Sensory Diet

Provide heavy work opportunities (proprioception) as suggested on above listed website pages

Fidgeting, distractibility

Try this:

- Offer a fidget toy to have at the desk such as:
  - Squeeze ball
  - Koosh or rubber band ball
  - Velcro (loop or hook) stuck underneath desk edge for fidgeting/rubbing with fingers

- Water bottle at desk to suck/drink
- Small piece of Theraband to pull/tug
- Tie Theraband around the front chair legs so the student can push against it with legs
- Allow student to stand at desk and work
- Oral snack throughout the day
- See Sensory Diet above
- Desk carrel for focused time
- Set a timer for work completion (not digital)
- Allow for movement breaks

Copying from board or overhead

Try this:

- Provide copy of notes
- Provide copy of notes for near point copying (on desk)
- Place colored overlay on overhead for better visual contrast
- Allow the student to come closer to the board
- Provide partial notes for fill in the blank rather than having to copy the entire text
- Provide copy of notes and have the student highlight key words

Copying notes—near point (from desk)

Try this:

- Provide copy of notes and have the student highlight key words
- Provide partial notes for fill in the blank rather than having to copy the entire text
- Allow the student to copy notes and exchange for teacher notes
- Teach the student outlining techniques
- If typing skills are adequate, allow for using a computer for note taking

Organizing school materials/desk

Try this:

- Use a desk organizer such as a Desk-A-Doo (www.deskadoo.com)
- Organize assignments and subjects in one notebook with different colored folders for subjects
- Use magazine holders at side of desk to hold books or folders
- Use pencil clip velcroed on the desk to hold pencil/pen
- Make labels with assignments pretyped for student to stick in his homework assignment book

Glossary

Bilateral Integration – The coordinated use of the two sides of the body to accomplish a functional task.

Bimanual Hand Use – The use of both hands in a lead-assist relationship.

Crossing Midline – The ability to spontaneously cross over the middle of the body.

Developmental Strokes – Prewriting strokes that include horizontal and vertical lines, a cross, and a circle.

Distal – Farthest from the center. "Distal fingers" means at the fingertips as opposed to at the palm.

Extrinsic Muscles – Larger muscles of the hand which attach at the elbow and cross the wrist. These muscles primarily offer stability.

Graded Activity – An activity that can be made more difficult or easier through adaptations and changes.

Hand Arches – The transverse and longitudinal arches of the hand which indicate proper hand development; strength, and stability.

Hand Separation – The development of two different sides of the hand—one side (pinky and ring finger) side offers stability, while the other (thumb, index, and middle) offer mobility and manipulation skills.

Hypothenar Eminence – The muscle belly of the little finger.

Intrinsic Muscles – The small muscles of the hand that attach within the hand. These muscles offer precision mobility as well as stability.

Kinesthetic – The sense of movement.

Motor Planning – The ability to move through a novel motor task without difficulties and transfer learned movement patterns to new tasks.

Motor Sequencing – Performing motor tasks steps in the proper order and with efficient timing.

Neurological Tract – Pathways of the nervous system.

Palmer Grasp – A crude grasp where the child holds the implement in the palm of the hand and wraps his fingers around the item in a fisted grasp.

Pincer Grasp – The ability to hold a small item between the thumb and index finger at the fingertips.

Pronation – Rotating the forearm so that the hand faces down.

Proprioception – The sense of body position in space through pressure in the joints.

Proximal Stability – The ability to maintain a fixed posture without external support, i.e., sitting in a chair. "Proximal" means toward the center of the body.

Seriation – The cognitive skill of ordering items according to qualities.

Shoulder Girdle – The muscles of the shoulder and scapula.

Somatosensory – The interpretation of tactile, vestibular, and proprioceptive input.

Splinter Skill – An isolated skill that is learned through rote, situational, and specific training.

Stereognosis – The ability to identify items and qualities of items by touch alone.

Supination – Rotating the forearm so that the hand faces up.

Tactile Discrimination – The ability to discriminate tactile qualities.

Thenar Eminence – The muscle belly of the thumb.

Thumb/Finger Opposition – The ability to bring the thumb toward the fingers and hold items. Essential for holding writing implements and for precision skills.

Translation skills – Moving small items from the palm of the hand to the fingertips with one hand. Also, rotation items across the fingers, from index to pinky with one hand.

Tripod Grasp – Using the index, thumb, and middle finger in a triangle-type grasp to hold a pencil or marker.

Trunk – Central part of the body, the core of the body.

Visual Perception – The ability to see, discern, and recognize shapes visually.

Visual-Motor Skills – The ability to draw or reproduce what one sees.

Wrist Extension – The position of the wrist for optimal hand function. The wrist is slightly bent up or extended.

Resources

Fun and Function – www.funandfunction.com
- A great resource at reasonable prices. Owned by an Occupational Therapist.

Therapro – www.therapro.com
- Excellent source of therapeutic fine motor activities and manipulatives and adapted materials
- Benbow scissors, squeeze scissors, and a variety of pencil grips
- Get-A-Grip-On Patterns Pegboard
- Wikki Stix and Activities
- Start Right and Grotto Pencil Grips
- Self-Opening (spring-loaded) Scissors
- Children's Learning Scissors (similar to Benbow scissors)
- *Loops and Other Groups*—cursive writing program by Mary Benbow, OTR

The Therapy Shoppe – www.therapyshoppe.com
- A growing source of fine motor and OT items

Pocket Full of Therapy – www.pfot.com
- Source for tongs

Lakeshore Learning – www.lakeshorelearning.com
- Educational manipulatives

Abilitations – www.abilitations.com
- Items specifically for children with disabilities.

School Specialty – www.schoolspecialty.com
- Offers discounts for schools that have contracts with the company. Pegboards, easels, Wikki Stix, and chalkboards.

Discount Teacher Supply – www.earlychildhood.com

U.S. Toy – www.ustoy.com
- Small items to pick up with tweezers—Koosh balls, mini-erasers
- Water squeeze toys

Chalkboard Contact paper is available through Amazon.com

Bibliography

Benbow, M. (2003). *Neurokinesthetic Approach to Hand Function and Handwriting.* Workshop presentation and workbook; Advanced Rehabilitation Institutes, Rocky Mount, North Carolina.

Bergmann, Kerstin P. (1990*).* Incidence of atypical pencil grasps among nondysfunctional adults *American Journal of Occupational Therapy,* 44, (736–740).

Berninger, Virginian W., & Rutberg, Judith (1992). Relationship of finger function to beginning writing: application to diagnosis of writing disabilities *Developmental Medicine and Child Neurology,* 34, (198–215).

Breslin, D. M. M., & Exner, C. E. (1999). Construct validity of the in hand manipulation test: a discriminate analysis with children without disability and children with spastic diplegia. *American Journal of Occupational Therapy,* 53, (381–386).

Burton, A., & Dancisak, M. (2000). Grip form and graphomotor control in preschool children. *American Journal of Occupational Therapy,* 54, (9–17).

Case-Smith J. & Pehoski, C. (1992). Development of Hand Skills in the Child. Rockville, MD: *American Occupational Therapy Association.*

Case-Smith, Jane (2002). Effectiveness of school-based therapy intervention or handwriting. *American Journal of Occupational Therapy,* 56, (17–25).

Cornhill, H., & Case-Smith, J. (1996). Factors that relate to good and poor handwriting *American Journal of Occupational Therapy,* 50, (732–739).

Daly, Christopher J., &Kelley, Gail T., &Krauss, Andrea (2003). Relationship between visual-motor integration and handwriting skills of children in kindergarten: A modified replication study. *American Journal of Occupational Therapy,* 57, (459–462).

Dennis, J.L., & Swinth, Y. (2001). Pencil Grasp and Children's handwriting legibility during different-length writing tasks. *American Journal of Occupational Therapy,* 55, (175–183).

Dryer, S.K. (1991). A Multisensory Approach to Handwriting Instruction. *OT Week,* 5, (14–15).

Elliott J. M., & Connolly K. J. (1984). A classification of manipulative hand movements *Developmental Medical Child Neurology,* 26, (283–296).

Erhardt, R. P. (1994). *Developmental Hand Dysfunction; Theory, Assessment and Treatment.* San Antonio, TX: Therapy Skill Builders.

ERIC Digest (1997). Six Questions Educators Should Ask before Choosing a Handwriting Program.

Exner (1990) The zone of proximal development in in-hand manipulation skills of nondysfunctional 3- and 4-year-old children. *American Journal of Occupational Therapists* 44, (884–891).

Fisher, A. G., Murray, E.A., Bundy, A.C. (1991) *Sensory Integration; Theory and Practice.* Philadelphia, PA: F.A. Davis Company.

Graham, S. (1992). Issues in Handwriting Instruction. *Focus on Exceptional Children, 25,* (1–12).

Henderson, A., & Pehoski, C. (2006). *Hand Function in the Child: Foundations for Remediation.* St. Lois, MO: Mosby-Year Book.

Jenkins, D. (2002). *Hollingshead's Functional Anatomy of the Limbs and Back.* Philadelphia, Pennsylvania 19106: W.B. Saunders Company.

Konnikova, M. (2014*).* What's Lost as Handwriting Fades. *New York Times.* June 3, 2014; Page D1.

Schneck, C. (1991) Comparison of Pencil Grip Patterns in First Graders With Good and Poor Writing Skills. *American Journal of Occupational Therapy, 45,* (701–704).

Vreeland, E. (1998). *Handwriting: Not just in the Hands; A Comprehensive Resource.* Hanover, NH: Maxanna Learning Systems.

Weil, M.J., & Cunningham Amundson, S.J. (1994) Relationship between visuomotor and handwriting skills of children in kindergarten. *American Journal of Occupational Therapy,* 48, (982–988).

Zaner-Bloser. (2000) *Handwriting Research and Resources; A Guide to Curriculum Planning.* Columbus, OH: Zaner-Bloser.

Ziviani, J. & Elkins, J. (1986). Effect of Pencil Grip on Handwriting Speed and Legibility. *Educational Review, 38,* (247–257).

Made in the USA
Monee, IL
13 August 2021